Drop Zone Burma

Drop Zone Burma

Adventures in Allied Air Supply
1942 – 45

Roger Annett

Pen & Sword
AVIATION

First published in Great Britain in 2008 by
Pen & Sword Aviation
an imprint of
Pen & Sword Books Ltd
47 Church Street
Barnsley
South Yorkshire
S70 2AS

ISBN 9781844157501

Typeset in Palatino Linotype by
Lamorna Publishing Services

Printed and bound in England by CPI

Pen & Sword Books Ltd. incorporates the imprints of Pen & Sword
Aviation, Pen & Sword Family History, Pen & Sword Maritime, Pen & Sword
Military, Wharncliffe Local History, Pen & Sword Select, Pen & Sword
Military Classics, Leo Cooper, Remember When, Frontline Publishing and
Seaforth Publishing.

For a complete list of Pen & Sword titles please contact
PEN & SWORD BOOKS LIMITED
47 Church Street, Barnsley, South Yorkshire, S70 2AS, England
E-mail: enquiries@pen-and-sword.co.uk
Website: www.pen-and-sword.co.uk

Contents

Acknowledgements

This is the story of eleven British young men, and one young woman, from a variety of backgrounds who were fated to rely on each other for survival in the extraordinary circumstances of warfare in the jungles of Burma. This five-year campaign was the longest in the Second World War and at over 5,500 miles from Britain, just about the most remote. Following the Allies' disastrous retreat and defeat in 1942, liberation of Burma and victory over the Japanese invader came, after much valiant effort and sacrifice, in 1945. Military analysts have concluded that the campaign itself, let alone the ultimate success, would hardly have been possible, in that most inhospitable of terrains, without air supply. This book is dedicated to the airmen who flew those missions, the groundcrew who kept the aircraft flying and the troops who were supplied – in the world's worst weather and against the most implacable of enemies.

In *A Short History of Nearly Everything* Bill Bryson writes: 'We are here only because for nearly four thousand million years our ancestors have managed to slip through a series of closing doors every time we needed them to.' In those years in Burma there were any number of closing doors. I have been privileged to meet some of our more adventurous British ancestors who against all the odds, managed to slip through.

My heartfelt thanks go first and foremost to those twelve veterans who freely gave their time and shared their memories in the preparation of this book. I am more than grateful to Tony Stephens, John Leary and the late Henry Probert for their help with references and records, and also to Seb Cox and his

colleagues at the RAF Air Historical Branch, Squadron Leader
Al Pinner and the staff at the Battle of Britain Memorial Flight,
and the Editor of *Star News*, Ian Hall. I am indebted to Dame
Vera Lynn and Viscount Slim for kindly contributing the preface
and foreword, and to my wife, Jenny for her patient support and
skilful editing of the text.

Roger Annett
April 2008

Foreword

by

The Rt. Hon. The Viscount Slim, OBE, DL
President, Burma Star Association

No one who fought in Burma has ever denigrated the courage of the Japanese soldier, sailor or airman. It can be argued that our Nation has never fought such a tough, tenacious, vicious and brave foe. It was his habits we hated towards those he conquered, his treatment of wounded and particularly of military and civilian prisoners of war.

The Fourteenth Army, the largest army of the Second World War, was made up of many races and all religions and it produced the leadership, spirit and guts to win.

The great lesson to emerge from this, the harshest of Campaigns, was the near total integration of Army and Air Force. The Army Commander and Air Marshal Baldwin's Third Tactical Air Force and Brigadier General Old's Joint American and British Troop Carrier Command all worked and lived together pooling intelligence and operational planning. The enormous difficulties overcome and the successes won on the Burma Front were a joint achievement.

I am so glad that the Author has included a Preface by Dame Vera Lynn. She is loved and admired by all who fought in Burma and is still today very much amongst us all in the family of the Burma Star Association.

It is only right that the Author in this competent and lively book brings us down to earth with the evidence of those who participated and fought at ground level.   Most of these wonderful and special men and women are known to me through our unique comradeship within the Burma Star. Like my father I am so proud of them all and wish this book and its Author every success.

SLIM
House of Lords
June 2008

Preface by Dame Vera Lynn DBE

In the New Year of 1944, when I approached ENSA with the suggestion that I might offer my services in entertaining Allied troops, it seemed to me that their lists were already pretty full, except for the so-called, even at that time, 'forgotten' campaign in Burma. We knew in London that the Japanese had invaded Burma in 1942, and that our troops had retreated into India to lick their wounds. We'd read a little in the papers about the bravery of the 'Chindits' and their guerilla expedition behind enemy lines. But it was the war closer to home that attracted most of the attention – and the stage and screen stars. I decided that I had better go where no one else had been before, and plumped for Burma.

A glance at the atlas showed me Burma, over 5,000 miles away, on the other side of India. Up to then the furthest abroad I'd been was the Dutch seaside, and I'd never flown, so I had a few butterflies at the thought. The British government also had their doubts about whether I should go. They thought I might harm the troops' morale by making them homesick. But I knew that my radio shows, broadcast to the boys and girls in the services, and to the people in occupied Europe, were very popular. So they were persuaded, and I went.

What an adventure it was. At the age of just twenty-seven, I left my new husband behind, and travelled for two weeks, mostly in a troop-carrying Sunderland flying boat, to Indian Assam. With my courageous pianist Len Edwards, and his trusty mini piano, I travelled most of the Burma front, and sang to many thousands of troops or sometimes to just a couple or so in the field hospitals. The air force and the army took such good care of us that despite the enemy, the rain and heat, and the mosquitoes, we survived. The boys told us we were good for morale. The very fact that we had come, and stayed for three months, showed them they were not, after all, forgotten back home. I wouldn't have missed that trip for the world.

I am therefore more than pleased to have been asked to write a preface for *Drop Zone Burma*. There can never be too many words written commemorating the heroism of the 'Burma Stars'. It took a lot of blood and sweat from the Allies until in August 1945 the Japanese were driven out of Burma. Many of the boys I sang to did not come home. Their memory has been honoured over the years at the annual Burma Campaign celebrations, and deservedly so. As this book shows, those sailors, soldiers and airmen were mostly ordinary citizens of Britain and the Commonwealth, caught up in a terrifying jungle conflict against a brutal enemy. As an ordinary citizen too, from Barking, I felt myself privileged to have been given the chance to do my bit.

Dame Vera Lynn DBE, LL.D, M.Mus.
Ditchling, East Sussex
10 November 2007

Prelude

Dakota over the Fens

Lincolnshire is at its best today – dark brown earth, silvery water and a hint of gold in the early autumn leaves. Down in the Thames Valley this morning, the weather looked promising, and it's stayed that way up the A1. But you never can tell with Lincolnshire. Dirty weather can blow in at any time off the North Sea, or creep down from the Yorkshire moors, up from the Fenlands, or over the Pennines. And fair weather is a must today. I'm due to go flying – in a Dakota, the workhorse transport of the British and American aircrews who flew thousands of air supply sorties in the Second World War Burma Campaign.

I turn east at Colsterworth, onto the B-road that becomes Ermine Street, the earliest of the arrow-straight military highways the Romans left in the region. It runs through Ancaster, where Tony Robinson and his *Time Team* uncovered an ancient Roman encampment. The British had bases all over Burma, but it's unlikely today's Burmese spend much time digging up the huts and latrines of the Allied Fourteenth Army.

From here to the Lincoln Edge twenty miles to the north, and the wolds over by the sea thirty miles to the east, there's hardly a hill in sight. In the Second World War, this flat county, located about as close to the enemy coast as you could get, was virtually one enormous air base. Most of the airfields are now mushroom farms and industrial estates but RAF Coningsby is still very much operational – it's the home of the Battle of Britain Memorial Flight, which operates a Dakota. It's where I'm heading today.

There's a window of settled weather and hopes are high for

Dakota-friendly conditions. With this flight, there'll be a chance of sharing something of what was experienced by the airmen and soldiers who served in the Burma Campaign and perhaps I'll be just that bit better qualified to record the stories being told me by some of those remarkable men.

Past Sleaford, the road to Coningsby runs along dykes around the fens, first drained for agriculture and then frequently requisitioned for wartime airfields. They bring to mind the paddy fields of Burma, drained in their turn by the Japanese and the advancing British Army for forward dirt airstrips. Bridges carry the road over waterways, as those built by Sappers in the steamy Burmese heat carried Allied tanks over rivers to the open plains.

Burma is driven out of my head by the sudden, ear-splitting thunder of a pair of Typhoon F2s running in to break, at low level. Five Mach 2 Typhoon squadrons operate from Coningsby and the howl of their engines is never far away, often joined by the racket of the Tornados and vertical take-off Harriers also based here.

Close by all that airborne muscle stands the BBMF hangar. A notice by the gate reads: 'Battle of Britain Memorial Flight Visitor Centre – a unique arrangement between Lincolnshire County Council and the Royal Air Force.' It's good to see that there is still a close relationship between the RAF and the people of this county.

The BBMF has celebrated its Golden Jubilee this year, 2007, and since the spring, its display Lancaster, Spitfires and Hurricanes have had scarcely a day off. But now, in October, they are in the hangar with their feet up, so to speak, their venerable airframes and engines being given some tender loving care by the fitters. The Dakota transport, however, flies on in the autumn. Acquired by the BBMF in March 1993, its main task is to give the Lancaster pilots time on a multi-engined, tail wheel aircraft before tackling the mightier bomber. But as a support aircraft to the team it's caught the eye of the crowds and now displays in its own right.

With coffee and a bun from the tea van, I settle down at a trestle table in the fresh air to await developments. There's the

Dakota – MkIII, airframe number ZA947 – on the hard standing outside the hangar doors. It's in camouflage colours, with 267 'Pegasus' Squadron markings. Corporal Clegg of the servicing crew told me on an earlier visit that it's had a new coat of paint.

'It was built in March 1942,' he said, 'but the aluminium skin was still in good condition. All the same, the job took a whole week – they had to strip off fourteen old layers.'

He told me that its wartime service with 267 Squadron was in the re-supply of troops and partisans in the Balkans, Middle East and Mediterranean in 1943 and 1944. From February 1945 the Squadron also served in Burma, but apparently without ZA947.

'Then it flew in the '48 Berlin Airlift and when it was done up for the BBMF, they had to clean out a whole lot of coal dust from under the freight floor.'

Fair weather cumulus clouds are building here and there, and nervously I recall that they don't fly the old Dakota in the wet – a bit of a change there from Burma. Groups of visitors file in and out of the hangar, led by volunteer guides in their military blazers and grey flannels, BBMF ties and gold badges.

Suddenly, there's activity on the hard standing. Groundcrew are plugging in the generator and swinging the props. Aircrew come out from the hangar, circle the aircraft for their external checks and climb aboard. Minutes later, a gloved hand from the cockpit window gives the thumbs up and there's the electronic whirr of a heavy-duty starter motor and the starboard propellor cranks over. The cylinders fire and the pungent oily smell of a petrol-driven piston engine wafts down to my table. Is this a warm up for flight or just an engine test? There had been talk of trouble with a magneto. The other engine starts. It runs sweetly for a minute, then the prop winds down – and the engine stops.

They try again. This time it keeps going, and after a few minutes' warm up, the chocks are waved away. The engine note rises, the prop wash stirs up the dust and the Dakota moves forward – and suddenly stops. Just testing the brakes. It taxis away. It's going flying.

On my mobile I call BBMF Operations and tell them I'm here. The operations assistant, Di Holland, comes to shepherd me through the cavernous hangar with another distinctive smell of oil and 100-octane aviation fuel. Spits and Hurricanes stand like tethered hawks in rows along the walls and at the far end looms the menacing shape of the Lancaster bomber.

'The Dakota is just off to the National Arboretum in Staffordshire,' Di tells me. 'The Queen's opening the new veterans' memorial and it's doing the fly past. It's due back in ninety minutes. Then they'll be doing two half-hour sorties to bring a couple of pilots to current on type. You'll be on the first of those.' That's what I wanted to hear.

Along the outside hangar wall are the flight offices and down the corridor is the crew room. It's comfortably furnished, with walls covered with photos, and cabinets full of trophies and mementoes. A nice place to wait, albeit nervously, for a Dakota sortie.

I see they've given me a waxed paper affair labelled: BAG, AIR SICKNESS NATO STOCK No 8105-99-130-2180. Having read about the Dak's tendency to bounce about in the air, I'm glad to have it. There's also an A4 photocopy of the 'Dakota Passenger Brief' which among other things says '...the rear door has been removed, so do not come further aft than the rear set of seats', but reassures that '...a safety harness will be fitted if you wish to stand in the door area'. You bet I do.

Fifteen other expectant aviators have arrived – a mix of serving men and women, and civilians from the supporting outfits on the station. We're led out to the grass by the hard standing, where the unmistakable beat of piston engines meets our ears. Back from its royal duty in Staffordshire, the Dakota's elegant airframe, sleek and neat against the building clouds, sails into view.

The practice circuits seem endless. Then, at last, around the corner of the Typhoon dispersal, tail wheel on the ground and nose in the air, the Dakota rumbles to meet us.

It comes to a stop, beam on to our waiting group. The door opens, the steps are put in place and a flying-suited figure clambers down. It's a squadron leader and his name tag reads Marcus Lee.

'Good afternoon, ladies and gents. I'm your loadmaster for

this flight. We'll take you eight at a time. Let's go.'

The engines are still running and the props waft the warm autumn air towards us. We heave ourselves up the ladder hooked onto the door sill, the first rung a good 3-feet stride up from the ground, and clatter up the steeply-sloping freight cabin floor. The aircraft is in paratroop dropping rig – continuous metal bucket seats with shoulder-to-shoulder seating for eight on either side. I'm given a headset and can hear the crew, perched up in front, running through the taxi checks. When they get to 'Tail wheel unlocked – Chocks away', the pilot opens the throttles, the throbbing of the engines intensifies and the aircraft moves forward. The 14-feet variable-pitch props thrum as the Dakota rolls past the parked Typhoons.

At the end of the runway the pilot turns into wind, puts on the brakes and runs up the engines to full power. The whole airframe throbs. He checks temperatures and pressures, and the magnetos by switching off each in turn and making sure that the revs don't drop more than they should. After generator and slow-running checks, the tail wheel is unlocked again. We're ready for take-off.

The pilot calls the tower and gets clearance. This is it. Turning onto the runway, over the earphones come more checks: 'Trimmers – Throttle friction – Mixture rich – Gills closed'. Then it's 'Full power' and we're off.

Did the troops and aircrew in Burma feel this same exhilaration on take-off? Engines strong and steady, tail lifting up, the Dakota's going like a train. The co-pilot calls 'Decision speed', and at about 60 knots, we're airborne. 'Undercarriage up', from the pilot and the landing gear lifts smoothly into recesses on the engine nacelles. We climb easily, the engine note changing as the pilot throttles back for the cruise.

What would all this have meant to lads scarcely out of their teens, more than sixty years ago? Imagine if we'd just flown off from a 600-yard Chindit strip with a full load of casualties, jungle in the windscreen and Jap small arms fire under our belly…

We head out over the fens of Lincolnshire.

Standing up I find that the cabin roof is about six inches above my head – that means it's some seven feet high, and about the same across. With eight people it's crowded. They packed in seventeen when a Dakota of 31 Squadron flew sick and wounded out of a jungle clearing on the first Chindit expedition. Half a dozen mules at a time were frequently transported, in bamboo pens. And on a mercy flight from Japanese-surrounded Myitkyina airfield it took all the refugees they could squeeze in.

Up front, the crew compartment reeks of warm leather, oil, electrics, fuel and old vomit. Immediately on the left is the navigator's station. In this cramped position they dead reckoned their way across the wildernesses of Burma, with no radio aids to speak of and in the most appalling weather. On the right is the wireless operator's position. In the Second World War there would have been a table there, with a Morse key and the code books. It's a storage space now – no one uses Morse any more, but in Burma it was a lifeline.

A radome in the cockpit roof is where the navigator stood to make his star shots, provided the cloud cleared enough to see them. On the left is an escape hatch, doubling as a crew entrance door when the load blocked the way through the freight cabin. It is just – dangerously just – in front of the port propeller.

There's no spare room behind the pilots. The bulk of two BBMF officers fills the seating space, which is not much more than you'd get in a family car. In the captain's seat is Flight Lieutenant Ed Straw and in the other, at the controls, is Squadron Leader Jeff Hesketh, a navigator being checked out for currency on type. On the central pedestal stand the throttle, mixture and flap levers, and prop pitch controls. To the left of the pedestal sits the substantial wheel for elevator trim. There's another escape hatch in the roof between the pilots and four sliding windows in the v-shaped windshield. The instruments show that we're flying at 120 knots at 1,200 feet, and the engines are running at 2,250 revolutions per minute. The control columns, one per side, are slim three-quarters wheels with thumb transmit buttons. The aircraft winds round into a turn, for all its 95-feet wingspan responding almost as well as a fighter. This airframe was state-of-the-art in 1943.

The expanse of the Wash comes up ahead. The muddy gullies and creeks of the Welland estuary stretch out below, possibly not unlike the sandbanks of Burma's Irrawaddy river, or the dropping zone on the shores of Lake Indawgwi. The port wing dips again and the Dakota swoops up towards the sands of Skegness, the gentle undulations of the Lincolnshire Wolds rising up to port. All's going very smoothly. Out in Burma, in moments of utmost peril – under attack from enemy fighters, being peppered with ground fire, or flying over mountains through towering thunderclouds – was the cockpit as calm and professional as this one? Or was it a capsule of sheer terror?

A tap on the shoulder tells me it's my turn to stand in the rear door, and I move carefully over the freight cabin floor with its load-tethering fitments. The formers are exposed all round and make good handholds. The fuselage walls and roof are aluminium, painted green. The loadmaster stands me under a steel cable running the length of the cabin ceiling. From it hangs a green webbing strap and a safety harness which is buckled tightly round my waist. Edging my way towards the door and the open sky I draw myself together and, grasping the frame with both hands above my head, plant my feet in the door sill and lean forward. The slipstream tugs at my clothes and hair and buffets my eyes and ears. The pilot throws the Dakota into a steep left-hand turn and there's a heart-stopping view of the mud banks of Anderby Creek down below.

The dispatch crews in Burma worked at this door sill for an hour at a time, sortie after sortie, pushing and kicking out 100lb harness packs of food, bullets and fuel on their heavy parachutes, and chucking out 50lb bags of rice or soya, often under fire. And when not jolted in monsoon turbulence and drenched by pouring rain, being choked with dust in the intense heat as the seasons changed. For this glimpse into the world of a dispatcher, I'm grateful.

Back in the circuit at Coningsby the crew run through their pre-landing checks, and the slipstream note changes as the undercarriage winds down and locks. The buildings of the air base slip by below and the Typhoons taxi out for a late afternoon mission, chunks of titanium and technology contrasting with this graceful collection of aluminium and rivets swooping over them to land.

The tyres kiss the tarmac and the aircraft rolls along, still with its tail in the air. As the speed drops off, the tailwheel sinks onto the runway, and we're down.

Rumbling back to dispersal, I think of the dozen veterans of the Burma Campaign I've had the privilege of meeting. Now I've flown in the Dakota – the vital link on which their survival depended – I'm encouraged to tell their stories, and feel better equipped to do them justice.

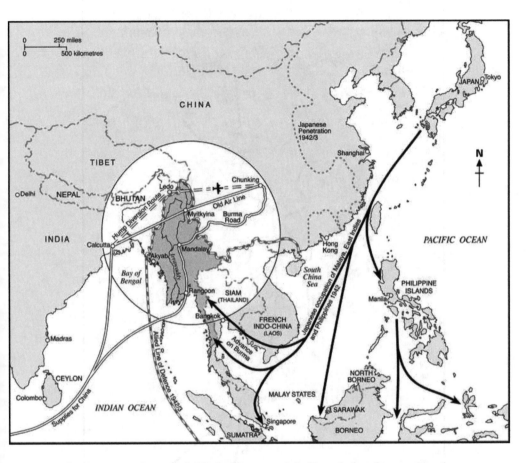

The Japanese Imperial High Command believed that by conquering Burma they would cut off the last supply route to China and protect their vast conquests in the south-west Pacific. The possibility also existed for further gains westward into India.

They also believed that mountains and jungles would set the Allies an impossible task should they attempt to reconquer Burma from bases in India to the north.

Courtesy of Michael Pearson

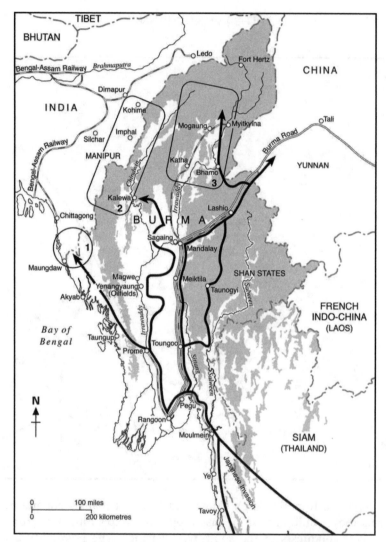

Key. The three fronts along which battle lines stabilized:
1. The Arakan.
2. The Central Front around Imphal.
3. Northern Combat Area Command.

Courtesy of Michael Pearson

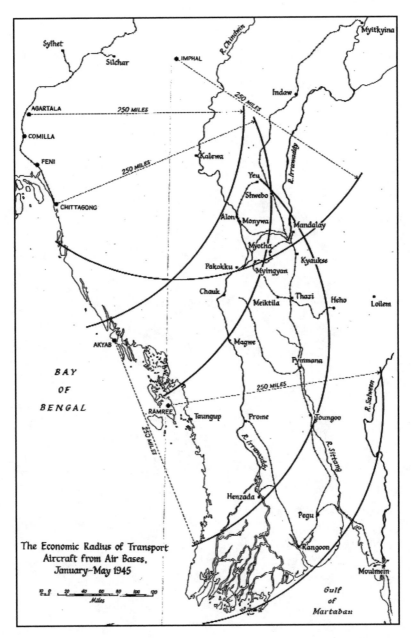

The Economic Radius of Transport
Aircraft from Air Bases,
January–May 1945

Courtesy of Arthur Watts

Chapter 1

Meet the Troops – and a Trouper

John Hart was born in 1921 in Rotherhithe, on the banks of the River Thames in East London. He was a machine operator up-river at Oxo when war broke out. All was pretty quiet until the summer of 1940:

'Then the Battle of Britain started, and all hell let loose. I was down in Kent that summer, picking hops. Out of nowhere a Junkers roars across – it's in flames, and being chased by a Spitfire. It crashes in the next field and blows up. As if that ain't enough to put the wind up you, there's the stray bullets from the dog-fights. I'm up in the vines when there's a scream from a woman in the next row. She drops off her ladder, stone dead.'

In 1939, during the 'phoney war', they'd read about the bombing of Warsaw:

'That was sort of unreal, and we didn't think it could happen in London. So, when the siren goes – 7th September it was – me and my mates think it's just another false alarm. We run out into the street to watch the aeroplanes. I can see them now, coming up the river. Then there's a great crash and a whoomph just up the road, and another and another – on and on – the first bombs of the Blitz, falling on the Surrey Docks. We scarper. From then on, it's every man for himself.

'Terrible it was. The fire at the timber warehouses burned from end to end – a mile long. Then, those bloody great landmines came floating down on their parachutes. On my way to work I see one blow up the signal box at London

Bridge station. Then another takes out the Town Hall just across the road from our flats. One night, another one knocks out thirty houses in one go in St Martin's Crescent along in Bermondsey. A pal of mine, away in the army, lost his whole family in that one – all ten of them.'

John's aunt and her family were bombed out:

'They'd set up a refuge centre in a local school. They're on the way to spend the night there but then they run across my other aunt, Theresa, who says, "Don't go down there – come and put up with us." So they did. That night the school gets bombed – and 300 die.'

John Hart was to be called up on his twentieth birthday, to serve as an RAF aircraftman in one of the most bitter battles of the Burma Campaign, the siege of Imphal.

On the other side of the river from John, fourteen year old Eric Knowles, out shopping in Ilford with his mother, also had a grandstand view of the German bombers coming up the Thames:

'There was an enormous pall of black smoke drifting all the way down the estuary as far as Southend. At night the base of the smoke cloud was bright red with the flames. The Blitz on London went on like that for fifty nights.'

The basements of the big stores in Ilford became air raid shelters. Eric's family had an Anderson in the garden, where they were joined by two uncles, two aunts and a grandmother who had been bombed out:

'One of the uncles and my father had been on the Western Front, and were singularly unimpressed by the Germans' efforts. They'd stand shaking a fist at the bombers and shouting, "Can't you do better than that, Gerry? You shot a bit straighter in the last lot!"'

The men of the family went fire watching, and often took the lad with them:

They had the soldier's knack of sleeping anywhere and would stretch out on the pews in the church, telling me to call them if there was anything happening.

He remembers a mass of contrails over Essex and Kent where the RAF was taking on the Luftwaffe:

'We could pick out the German aircraft. They were the ones in big formations, and their engines were unsynchronised and made this vroom-vroom noise. The bombing reached its climax with the Fire Blitz of the City at the end of December. My uncle took me to his printing works on Tower Hill and I saw the ruins for myself. I got a job in 1942, as a tape-room boy with the *Daily Mirror* in Fetter Lane. I was there for the May Blitz in 1943.'

Eric decided that he'd had enough and resolved to do something about it. Still only seventeen, he applied for service as a Boy Entrant in the army. He was to show up in Burma in 1944 with a Bren gun, fighting down the Ledo Road with the Royal East Kent Regiment – 'The Buffs'.

By the summer of 1940, Norman Currell was a twenty-six year old police sergeant stationed in Romford, five miles up the A12 from Eric Knowles:

'We were all very much aware of the Battle of Britain overhead – where I was stationed the air was full of bombers and fighters tearing into each other. Then came the Blitz.

From November 1940 until the following month of May, there were very few nights when we weren't subjected to a steady stream of German bombers. They only had to follow the River Thames up from Southend and then it was impossible to miss the docks at Grays in Essex and those further west, in London. We had a few narrow escapes from bombs being released before they got that far.

'My brother John and I were out one evening and on the way home, near the church in Hornchurch, we heard a plane coming towards us. We had a suspicion it was a Jerry, and we bloody well knew it was when he started dropping a line of bombs. Each one was getting closer than the one before – too ruddy close. One of them blew up in the churchyard, laid us flat out on the pavement, and showered us with earth. Fortunately, it was the last in the stick.'

Norman remembers an incendiary raid at the end of December:

'There was a steady ring of fire around the docks, all the way from London out to Grays. When we went out next day the ground was covered with charred Christmas cards, blown over from thousands of burning mantlepieces in the East End. That was one heck of a raid.'

When the bombing subsided later in 1941, Norman applied to join the RAF, became a pilot, and would find himself four years later posted to Burma on a Dakota squadron.

Born in 1914, also in the East End, Henry Stock was older than John and Eric. Married to Marjorie, he saw much of the action from the City, working as a solicitor's clerk with the Woolwich Building Society:

'A couple of months before the Blitz, out of my office window I'd seen the shot-up lads from Dunkirk down on the railway platforms below – poor blighters. I reckoned I'd be joining them soon. Then came the bombing to frighten us stiff. I thought, Better get out of this, quick.'

The Royal Sussex Regiment was reformed from those Dunkirk survivors, and strengthened by the 'Shiny 9th' Battalion, made up partly by Sussex men and partly by Londoners. Sure enough, later in 1940 Henry joined them. As a private in a signal platoon, along the mountain ranges from John Hart, he was to fight in the Battle of the Arakan.

Another Londoner who saw as much of the Blitz as anybody, was Vera Lynn, born in 1917 in East Ham. Just as the Battle of Britain was beginning in earnest in the summer of 1940, she opened in the revue *Applesauce* at the Holborn Empire:

'When the night bombing of London started in the autumn,

the shows in the West End kept going. People needed the laughter and glamour to keep their spirits up. On top of the air raids, I had to get to the theatre from my home in Barking in my little Austin Ten – and back again in the blackout.'

Vera was doing two shows a day, an afternoon performance and another in the evening:

'If there was an air raid warning they'd put a notice up by the stage saying so – but most of the audience would stay in their seats. You could more or less bet that if a bomb was to fall anywhere near – and they did – it would be in the middle of *A Nightingale Sang in Berkeley Square*, or a quiet number like that. If the raid got noisier, and was still going at the end of a show, the audience would stay in the theatre and we'd have a sing-song. We didn't get much sleep in those days.'

Then the Holborn Empire's luck ran out:

'I turned up for a matinee to find a notice on the stage door: Danger – Time-Bomb, it said. That put the lid on it. While the Empire was closed I took my Austin on the road, and put on shows at bases and barracks, and factories and hospitals as well. That was an adventure too, what with the roads crowded with convoys and me with just masked headlights on my little car. Some journeys were complete chaos – firemen, hosepipes and rubble everywhere. What should have been a thirty-minute drive would take me hours.'

The fates then decreed that the temporary closure of the Holborn Empire should become permanent. It took a direct hit:

'The whole place was flattened, and without that time-bomb, we'd have been there to get flattened too.'

Plans were made to move the revue to the Palladium:

'But then that got hit too. A landmine came through the roof and finished up hanging from its straps just above the stage. A few inches more and it would have taken out the theatre and a whole chunk of Oxford Street with it. That was another narrow escape.'

Applesauce eventually opened at the Palladium, in March 1941. Four months later, Vera went down with appendicitis, but after a tricky operation she recovered and was back on stage after only seven weeks:

'I reckoned I must just have been destined to survive the Blitz.'

She was also destined in March 1944, after many more months of morale-boosting record releases, shows and broadcasts as the Forces' Sweetheart, to appear onstage in a very different kind of theatre – the battlefields of Burma, bringing cheer to the likes of John Hart, Henry Stock, and all their mates in the Arakan.

Also in that battle was George Hufflett. The son of a blacksmith in Alciston, under the Downs in East Sussex, he was sixteen in 1940 and too young for call up – so he joined the Home Guard:

'Our base was in a searchlight outfit on the cricket field. At the start, apart from marching up and down with pitchforks and the like, we didn't do much more than fill sandbags for bomb shelters. But then the Battle of Britain started, and we had a grandstand view. Up there above the Downs, was a whole mess of contrails. You could see lines of bombers coming in and the fighters twisting and turning. A right racket it was. And you had to keep your head down with the burning planes falling out of the sky – cannon shells and jettisoned bombs too.'

Home Guard duties included patrolling in the blackout, checking for lights, fire watching and, on occasion, the dousing of incendiary bombs:

'One night, in the pitch dark, I took a tumble into this bloomin' great ditch – came home sopping wet. My mum didn't half tell me off. Another night an incendiary fell on The Cricketers pub at Berwick and they sent me off to get the local bobby. I ran all the way to his caravan, a mile or so away. But all he said was, "Can't you lads deal with it? Only the missus is out you see, and I'm looking after the dog." So I ran all the way back and we dealt with it.'

Within two years, George joined the ranks of the Royal Sussex and was to find himself, in late 1943, on a mountain side in the Arakan.

A dozen miles to the west of Alciston, Ken Brown, another sixteen year old, watched the fighters and bombers of 1940 from the heights behind the seafront in Brighton. Ken's father, a volunteer company officer in the National Fire Service, had a newsagent's in Kemp Town and the family lived over the shop:

'Brighton was in the front line for the invasion which we were expecting any day, and we were right underneath the Battle of Britain. There were fighters and bombers up there every day. We were also a pretty easy target for Jerry's cross-Channel raiders.'

He was working in the shop when he had his first brush with death:

'I'll never forget Saturday 14th September. I was standing behind the counter when I heard the roar of aero engines, really close. A split second later there was one hell of a wallop over the road, and the windows of our shop were blown in. I didn't have time to duck. The blast bowled me over and I had blood running down my face where the glass splinters hit me. I was sitting in the middle of a whole lot of smashed four-and-a-half-pound sweet jars, and remember thinking, Blimey, I'll have a job stopping the kids nicking this lot.'

He picked himself up and staggered out to the road:

'The bomb had landed on the other side of the street and had taken out the front wall of the house opposite. It was carnage. Me and some other fellers did what we could but one chap died right on our doorstep. Then I saw a girl all red on one side and blue on the other – it turned out she'd been splattered by two bottles of ink flying off the shelf. Gave me quite a turn.'

A policeman sent him off to hospital with glass embedded in his face, a small piece of bomb casing behind his left ear, and a hole in his glasses:

> 'It was my glasses that saved my sight. What a bit of luck. My dad told me the next day that it was a lone Dornier bomber, being chased by a Spitfire from Tangmere airfield. The Jerry pilot must have dumped his whole bomb load trying for maximum speed – twenty 100-pounders, all at once. Two of them fell on the Odeon cinema round the back – it was a children's matinee and four of them died. Another one fell in Rock Grove and three of one family copped it – all from different generations. Just like that – out of a clear blue sky. They reckoned over fifty poor blighters had had it.'

That all happened as the Battle of Britain was nearing its climax, but the raids on Brighton continued:

> 'It was called the Brighton Blitz. They mounted a Bofors gun in every shelter along the seafront.'

He was to endure another couple of years living on the edge, with more narrow escapes until, at the age of eighteen, he joined the Royal Signals. A year or so later he too, was to end up in Burma, ten miles or so from George Hufflett, at the siege of Kohima.

Arthur Watts, born in 1921 on a farm just a short stroll from Ken Brown, missed the Brighton Blitz. By 1940 he had left his apprenticeship as an engine fitter at Allen West Engineers and volunteered for the RAF. He was attested at Uxbridge and then sent up to Blackpool for technical training:

> 'The first weeks were about tool familiarisation. Now, I'd been working to fine limits with all sorts of tools at Allen West's and so I could help the instructors out. A lot of the recruits were ex-clerks and such and knew next to nothing about engineering.'

After six months of training, Arthur was posted, as a leading air-craftman airframe fitter, to Number 67 Maintenance Unit at Taunton, Somerset:

'The MU was just being set up. Four of us – warrant officer, corporal and two of us airmen – had our base at Marshall's Garage. Others arrived and we'd just enough for a working gang when the air battles started.

'We were put onto aircraft recovery and on our first day of duty, we had to go and pull the crew out of an aircraft that had crashed on the Lizard. Nasty work that. Didn't matter whether it was a friendly or a Jerry – the smell was always the same. And the exploding ammo had us jumping about, I can tell you.'

Arthur decided he had more to offer the war effort and volunteered for service overseas. He embarked at the end of 1942, sailed round the Cape to Durban, and then onwards to Bombay. After adventures on India's North-West Frontier, he volunteered again. This time it was for the Burma Front and in late 1943 he was posted as a corporal fitter to the Agatarla RAF base in Assam, from where 31 Squadron's Dakota transports were dropping supplies to George Hufflett and the boys in the Arakan.

Further on down the south coast, Portsmouth and Southampton were also feeling the heat of German air attacks. Two brothers, Derrick and Richard Hull were in the thick of it. Sons of a grocery chain manager, they'd moved around the country, finishing up in Bitterne, two miles east of Southampton, just in time for the arrival of the Luftwaffe.

Aged fourteen, Richard left school to join Southern Daily Newspapers, working in the *Daily Echo* office as general office boy. Derrick, three years older, had already started work, at Folland Aircraft, in the buying office:

'At that time, they had 4,000 working in the company. Most of the jobs were contracts for aircraft maintenance. Before 1938, you could see Imperial Airways flying boats, sometimes four at a time, taxiing up to the shore and being winched onto ramps for servicing.'

At eighteen, he joined the Home Guard:

'I was guarding the factory in the evenings, cycling five miles each way from home in the blackout, with my rifle and fifty rounds of ammo. Once, I was stopped by a policeman for not having lights on the bike. I tell him, "You can't get batteries – there's a war on." But he still books me. I got fined a hefty ten bob for that. I made sure at work that an order for batteries was put in pretty sharpish.'

Richard also has his own vivid memories of the early war years:

'There were always aircraft around on Southampton Water. We had not only Folland but also Armstrong Whitworth, Vickers Supermarine and Fairy. Then there were the oil and gas refineries, and the docks of course – all big targets for German bombers. Apart from those, the raiders targeted Millbrook Station, right in the centre of town. It took the first bombs of the war, in October '39, and when they started the night raids in 1940, a garage next to it just disappeared with the first stick. It was easy to find – they could line up on the white, 150 feet high clocktower of the Civic Centre.

'The bombers and fighters put on a pretty much non-stop show which fascinated me as a teenager. There were bits of flak and shell nose-caps lying around like litter – my chums and I collected them. Then one day, cycling home from the *Echo*, there was this Heinkel coming straight at me at tree-top level, going hell for leather after an attack on Hamble. The front gunner's face was staring out of the lower wind-screen, clear as day. He was strafing the railway line and I was in his line of fire. Bullets were smacking into the ground and ripping through the trees and fences. He missed me by a whisker – ruddy terrifying.

'Bombs hit the art college close by the *Echo*, and dozens of students were killed. Luckily, they just missed us, but a concrete block fell on my new bike and squashed it flat – my mate's was right next to mine but his wasn't touched. All I could think of was getting that ruddy concrete off my bike – but a copper pulled me off it and got me to the shelter. Probably saved my life. Funny, the things you do in air raids.'

The *Echo* office was evacuated, just in time, as on 30 November 1940 it was burned to the ground:

'I was sent up to London, to the *Echo*'s Fleet Street office – out of the frying pan and all that... Despite the raids I enjoyed London life. I lodged with a family in East Acton. In the office I was one of half a dozen admin staff and had a pretty responsible job for a sixteen year old. My mentor was an ex-bandmaster from the Durham Light Infantry, an Indian. I was pretty impressed by what he told us about his exploits in the Boer War and in India on the North-West Frontier. So as soon as I could, I joined up.'

Richard went into the RAF in 1943, aged eighteen. In tests at Euston House he did well in the radio section and after training at the Compton Bassett radio school, passed out as AC1 Wireless Operator with twenty-two words per minute Morse. He was sent to Lyneham for posting overseas, as reinforcements were needed for a big push in Burma. He arrived in the mountains on the Burma border, at Tulihal, just south of the main base at Imphal, in mid-1944.

His brother Derrick had already signed up in the RAF. He volunteered aged nineteen in April 1941, beating the call-up by three months:

'Otherwise, living in the heartland of the Senior Service, I would probably have been a cert for the Navy.'

He reported to Cardington, Bedfordshire, where he was given his uniform and kit:

'Then we went square-bashing on the seafront in Skegness until May – four weeks without a break. With the cookhouse a mile up the road we got plenty of exercise, and our flight sergeant was an ex-champion boxer, Tommy Reddington. He took us on five-mile runs. That sorted us out, literally – anyone who didn't make it round the course was never seen again.'

Derrick graduated in December 1941 as an AC1 Instrument

Repairer and was posted to 600 Beaufighter Squadron, night fighters, at Predannock, off Lizard Point in Cornwall:

> 'Jerry was still at it. I was on duty crew one night when a Dornier, closely followed by one of our fighters, came in low and dropped his stick of bombs. Fortunately they didn't do much damage, but they did shatter our peaceful existence. Right away I put down for overseas duties.'

His four-week embarkation leave was cut to just seven days (during which he got engaged to Vera) and he boarded the *Ormonde* for a three-week voyage round the Cape to Suez. After a challenging time with aircraft ferrying and delivery units in the heat of North Africa, at the turn of 1945 he was posted to the cold and wet of Bari in Italy. There, he heard that 267 Squadron, which was on the base with Dakotas, was bound for Burma and looking for volunteers. Derrick was first in line and in February he arrived, like his brother before him, at Tulihal.

By the time of the Battle of Britain, London-born Peter Bray was already an RAF pilot:

> 'In July 1940 I was at the Elementary Flying Training School at Ansty, five miles north-east of Coventry, as a Qualified Flying Instructor (QFI) on Tiger Moths. Coventry was certain to be a target for the Luftwaffe, being a major manufacturing centre. The first bombs fell on our airfield the month before I got there. Then in August, Jerry hit the town centre and left our favourite cinema, the Rex, in ruins. A month or two later a bigger raid killed nearly 200 and destroyed a hospital, and many of the inmates along with it.'

Worse was to come:

> 'On 14 November, about seven in the evening, over 500 German bombers came over. The racket of the engines brought us out of the mess to watch the parachute flares come down. With the flares they dropped incendiaries – horrible exploding phosphorus devices that stuck, burning, to buildings, trees and flesh alike. After half an hour the

main force arrived with high explosive bombs and a firestorm started in the centre of the city. The cathedral was alight before eight o'clock. We could hear the bells of the fire engines rushing to the city – ours from the station went too, but there wasn't much they could do. The flames were leaping a hundred feet into the sky. They'd dropped oil bombs too and the smoke from them was awful. The raid went on all night – the all clear didn't sound until after six in the morning.'

The devastation in Coventry was appalling – it was by far the heaviest raid on the UK of the war and the Luftwaffe came back at Easter 1941 to deliver two more, each about seven hours long. By then Peter had been posted to train bomber pilots, but he has a final memory of Ansty:

'A German invasion was expected at any time and the engineers fitted out our Tiger Moths with bomb-racks so that we could dive-bomb them. We practised with smoke bombs.'

Anyone who has flown the Tiger Moth will know the courage required even to consider diving low in a slow, un-armoured biplane, to mount an attack on a division of Panzers.

Eventually Peter's number came up for overseas duty and, in November 1942 (on his 23rd birthday), he set course in a brand new Wellington bomber for India. There, the wheel of fortune turned again, and he was transferred to Dakotas. On 14 March 1943, he reached Assam, to fly 31 Squadron's air supply missions over Burma.

Soon to join the same squadron was Colin Lynch. He too, had seen graphic scenes of the Battle of Britain and the Blitz, but in newsreels on Indian cinema screens. In September 1940, having been born and brought up in the British Raj, he was in his last year at school, where he and his classmates dreamed of becoming fighter pilots.

Early in life, he had seen Wapitis and Hawker Harts in action in north-west India, and got the flying bug. So, in December, after passing the Senior Cambridge Certificate at Grade One in nine subjects, he rejected the option of university and was selected and trained as an RAF aircrew observer.

The Harts that he had seen on the North-West Frontier were from 31 Squadron. He joined the same squadron, on their Dakotas, at Agartala in Assam in May 1943. Aged twenty, he was about to fly with the air drop crews, supplying the troops in Burma.

As for so many of the nation's people, the Battle of Britain and the Blitz gave these eleven young men and one young woman their first experience of the horrors of war. All of them were destined to play their part in the longest battle of that war, the Burma Campaign.

Chapter 2

First Burma Star

George Hufflett is the first to tell me the story of his time in Burma, but it takes a while for him to start. For more than thirty of the fifty years I'd known him he was a fixture behind the bar at the Ram Inn in Firle, a village lying below its beacon hill a couple of miles west of his birthplace. He ran the pub with his wife Mary, the licensee.

It was well known that he'd served in the war – when pulling pints he couldn't hide the scars along his gammy right arm. The regulars said it had been shot up by Japanese bullets – but he'd never wanted to talk much about it. Following his retirement, and now a widower, he could often be seen at weekends outside the pavilion under the trees, watching the cricket. After one match, an invitation is offered for a cup of tea at his flint and brick cottage alongside the war memorial at the top of the village.

Among the souvenir mugs and family photographs lies a row of medals, including the distinctive six-pointed Burma Star with its red, yellow and blue ribbon. George can see they've attracted my attention and he confides that he'd been a rifleman in the battles of the Arakan and Kohima at the turn of 1944, when the enemy was pressing forward, aiming to wrest control of the Burma-India border.

He knows I was in the RAF, albeit more than a dozen years after the war.

'We had your lot dropping bullets and bully beef to us on parachutes,' he says with a smile. 'Marvellous, that was.'

He hands over two articles recently printed from the Internet. A quick look through shows that one is from the Burma Star

Association and is about the Arakan, and the other tells of the four months of continuous direct contact with the enemy that he and his regiment had had in that engagement.

He starts to talk of how he came to be in Burma, first going back to his Sussex beginnings.

Next to youngest of five siblings, he lived with his family in a thatched cottage in Alciston, close by the ancient church with its landmark dovecot and tithe barn. When he was one year old, they moved round the corner to the white clapboard two-storied Forge Cottage, wedged between the Barley Mow pub and the seventeenth century brick-built forge:

> 'I wasn't very big but my father let me have a go at pumping the bellows and helping my brothers strap red-hot metal tyres on to the cartwheels. The wood didn't half scorch – lovely smell. They sent me to the parish school in Selmeston, over the Polegate road – there wasn't that much traffic then but you had to plough your way through the sheep.'

There were some fifty pupils – infants, juniors, and seniors up to the age of fourteen, under the care of three teachers, including the headmistress who lived alongside the schoolhouse. They went out to play on the cricket field, and for books they filed down to the reading room in the parish hall.

On Saturday mornings George earned two shillings digging in the local sandpits, and when he left school he took up this manual work fulltime:

> 'I wasn't really old enough but I made sure I got to drive the sandpit lorry – that came in useful later on.'

Shortly before his sixteenth birthday, war with Germany was declared and he and his mates started shovelling sand into bags for bomb defences. When he turned seventeen, he registered with Army Recruiting:

> 'The army office was in Hammond's Furniture Removals place up on Lewes High Street. I went there with my mate Fred Tingley, from the butcher's in Polegate. When we were walking back the sky was full of aeroplanes – dogfights all over.'

He had to wait two years, doing his duty in the Home Guard, before being called up at eighteen:

'In June 1942 I got a letter telling me to report to the Royal Sussex Regiment. We all knew what they used to say about them: Sussex men born and bred, strong in the arm and thick in the head. I was sent off to training camp at Tilehurst and signed on as private for the duration – for service anywhere. It was bloomin' lonely, right up there outside of Reading – first time away from home and none of the other Selmeston boys had been sent with me.'

After square bashing, the assault course, rifle drills and practise with grenades and 25lb bombs, he became an infantryman. Soon after Christmas 1942, the bunch of recruits was posted to Colchester, and then moved to Exeter. Some went abroad from there but the rest, in June 1943, were sent to Hartlepool on Teesside:

'I'd told them about my time with the sandpit lorry so I got to drive a fifteen hundredweight pick-up truck. That was a right old jaunt. We went straight through Cirencester and Brum in the blackout. It was pretty slow going and one night we camped right out in the middle of Doncaster racecourse. Peaceful it was there, under the stars.

In Hartlepool they settled down to wait for embarkation:

'They'd issued us with tropical kit, so we reckoned it had to be Burma.'

After two months, the Regiment went from Hartlepool by train to the Clyde, and filed onboard a medium-sized troopship:

'I forget the name, but only about 8,000 tons she was – not very comfortable and there wasn't a sick-bay. We sailed in a convoy with a destroyer escort – they buzzed up and down all over the place, after German U-boats. We went right out into the Atlantic to try and lose the blighters. One night, the ship broke down and when we woke up in the morning there wasn't another ship in sight. That was a bit of a worry, stuck in the middle of the sea all by ourselves, and quiet, like. It was a relief when the engines started up again – we were able to get a move on and catch up.'

The first landfall, after two weeks at sea, was Freetown on the west coast of Africa:

'We couldn't get off the boat but when we got out to sea again, I took sick. They found I had malaria – it must have been a mosquito that got at me in the harbour. I had a pretty rotten couple of weeks – all they could do was to dose me with mepacrine, which turns you yellow.'

As soon as they docked in Durban he was whisked off the ship and into hospital:

'It was my twentieth birthday. The treatment was much the same, but at least there was a proper ward to lie in and pretty nurses too.'

The convoy went on without him so he caught the next one:

'This ship was loaded with a West African division, the first black men I'd ever seen – a real eye-opener.'

After putting in at Mombasa on the coast of Kenya, in October his convoy arrived in Bombay:

'We couldn't see much sign of the war in Bombay. But there was a bloomin' great explosion when a big old freighter blew up. Turned out it was carrying hand-grenade explosive and the whole thing got catapulted onto the quay – lay there on its side with its bottom blown out.'

George arrived at his transit camp in Nasik, outside Bombay:

'They told me it was Gandhi's birthplace, but I didn't have time to look around. I'd missed the Royal Sussex transport, with all my pals in it – they'd been moved on. I was told to join up with the First Queen's, and to look sharp about it.'

The 1st Queen's was on its way to incorporation in the 7th

Indian Division, for reinforcement of the British Fourteenth Army, over on the eastern side of India, in Assam:

'We set off straight away on a train to Calcutta – two days it took. That's a trip I don't want to remember. It was pretty rough in the carriages and the toilet was just a great big old hole in the floor at the end – luckily, when we stopped, the locals brought us cans of water so we could wash our bums.'

The 1943 monsoon was delivering its final burst:

'There was lots of heavy cloud, wind and rain. It was chilly at night and when the train stopped to refuel we'd take a biscuit tin along to the engine, and boil water on the hot bits for tea. Once when it was my turn, a valve blew and flushed all the char out of the tin – the lads didn't take too kindly to that. We didn't have a lot of rations but we picked up a few chapattis from hawkers here and there. But we forgot all about that when we got to Calcutta and saw the famine. People were in a terrible state, thin as rakes, and there were bodies lying all over in the streets. It fair shook us up, I can tell you.

'We were glad to get out of it and climb on the next train – on the Bengal-Assam railway. It was a narrow gauge affair and it took us another two days to rattle a good way up the Ganges, along the Brahmaputra and then down the coast to Chittagong. We ended up about a hundred miles from the border with Burma – billeted all together in timber-framed huts. My word, it was a long way from Sussex. Our corporal said we were going off to fight the Japs in the Arakan.'

George's battalion were trucked as far as the metalled road down the Assam coast could take them:

'We foot-slogged it from Cox's Bazaar, the Naf River over on our right, the mountains on our left and the Japs in front – somewhere. The first day, after about twenty miles, the corporal said we'd crossed the border into Burma. We bivouacked that night, and next day we hiked over to the other side of the Mayu mountains through the Okeydoke Pass.

'Well, it was called something else in Burmese, but everyone called it Okeydoke. Anyway, it wasn't much of a road – bloomin' steep it was, and it took us all day. When we got down to the valley, the corporal said we were going to march on south, into enemy country, and attack some road tunnels held by the Japanese – all sounded a bit dangerous to me.'

George and I have covered enough ground for one evening. But of course, I want to know more. What happened next? Where exactly was the Arakan, what was state of the battle when he was there – and where was the 'Okeydoke' Pass?

Leaving him with thanks for the tea, and his agreement to my coming back for more, I set myself to do some homework on the Burma campaign.

Chapter 3

The Fall of Burma

Bentley Priory, near Stanmore in north London was the Headquarters of RAF Fighter Command in the Second World War. Did the station look then as it does now, with neat laurel hedges and white kerb stones? Two iconic fighters, a Spitfire and a Lightning, stand proudly on their pedestals in front of the turreted Officers' Mess. That's where the chief of Fighter Command, Lord Dowding may have stood (Laurence Olivier certainly did in *The Battle of Britain*) and watched London burning.

Opposite the Lightning, in a standard military two storied building, unimpressive in grey breeze block, is the RAF Air Historical Branch, known to its friends as the AHB. The Director, Seb Cox, and his staff have been of great help in the past and again they patiently allow me to spend several days buried in their archives, searching files and boxes packed with books, papers and pamphlets on the war in Burma.

The scale of the operation is a surprise. On the ground, around 100,000 British and Gurkha troops, 340,000 Indians, 90,000 West and East Africans, 65,000 Chinese and 10,000 Americans were ranged against a total of some 330,000 Japanese. In the air, forty-seven United States squadrons took part, alongside fifty-five British, four Australian, a couple from Canada and one from New Zealand. The Japanese Army Air Force operated a score of Flying Regiments. The battles were fought across a total area bigger than the European theatre, in a country larger than Germany. It was the longest campaign by far of the war and, for many British and Indian servicemen, the conflict went on until the end of 1946 in the Netherlands East Indies and other territories invaded by the Japanese.

The story had its beginnings in the 1930s. The Japanese, who had been sniping at China since the First World War, began running serious offensive operations there in 1931, occupying Manchuria and building up a base there for further invasion before, in 1937, engineering open war. Occupying large tracts of the country, their troops gained battle experience and a reputation for vicious ruthlessness, perhaps the worst example being the December 'Nanking massacre', when between 200,000 and 300,000 Chinese citizens were slaughtered by the Imperial Japanese Army.

On 22 September 1941, Japan signed a tripartite pact with Germany and Italy, and invaded French Indo-China, launching the drive to set up the cherished dream of a 'Great Co-Prosperity Regime'. They set out to commandeer the raw materials, especially oil, that were in scarce supply on their crowded, industrialised islands, and to challenge what they saw as the imperial yoke of the British, French, Dutch and Americans. On 7 December 1941, the United States Pacific Fleet's battleship force was wrecked by a Japanese air attack at Pearl Harbor in the Hawaiian island of Oahu. On the same day their troops landed in northern Malaya and the Philippines. Hong Kong and British Borneo fell the same month.

Ill-prepared, and with their main concentration in Europe and the Mediterranean, the odds were heavily against the defending colonial forces. There was some gallant resistance but, just three days after Pearl Harbor, Japanese bombers and torpedo-bombers sank the Royal Navy's *Prince of Wales* battleship and the battlecruiser *Repulse* off the east coast of Malaya.

Within two months the bulk of Malaya and all of Singapore fell and the invaders were poised on the Siam border with Burma. At the turn of 1942, three infantry regiments of the battle-hardened Japanese Fifteenth Army began their advance, aiming to close the Burma Road which ran from Rangoon, the capital and largest port, across the mountains to China. With Indian Ocean sea lanes closed by the Japanese fleet, this 1,000 mile road was the last remaining route for American Lend-Lease supplies to the nationalist forces opposing them in China. A further reason for going forward was to protect the conquests already made. And they weren't going to stop at Burma. Their grand plan was to invade India, kick the British out and link up with Fascist forces coming down through the Caucasus. They expected to finish off the British war effort and force the Americans into a negotiated peace.

At the time – two years of age in my playpen in Surrey – I had no idea of all this. I now wondered how much of it my father knew, in his destroyer gun turret, chasing U-boats in the Mediterranean. And what did George Hufflett think of it all, waiting for call up in Sussex? He must have read the headlines in the *Brighton Argus* as the Japanese advance swept on and on. He was not to know that he was going to be drawn into that faraway battle before he was twenty-one.

The Japanese evidently held all the cards. Their lines of communication (LOC) were stretched over 3,000 miles from Rangoon back to Tokyo, but they had the world's third largest navy, concentrated in the Pacific, to protect their shipping lanes. They had carriers flying the Mitsubishi Zero fighters, whose effectiveness had taken even the Americans by surprise. The British Eastern Fleet was massively outgunned by the Japanese First Carrier Fleet and had been chased from its Calcutta and Ceylon bases to the relative safety – but frustrating remoteness – of East Africa. On top of all that, in Indo-China, Siam and Malaya, they had occupied air bases that brought Burma within the range of their air forces, and their combat proven pilots.

And what was the RAF doing about the Japanese advance? The remnants of their gallant but doomed squadrons, operating their obsolescent aircraft out of Singapore, had been scattered to the Indonesian islands of Sumatra and Java and then, as they were overrun by the end of May, were chased to Australia and Ceylon. To the British and Indian troops in the firing line, the RAF offered only token air cover.

All this was desperate for the defenders of Burma. Lines of supply over the Bay of Bengal were under intense threat from the enemy on the sea and in the air, and there were none overland, for there was precious little communications infrastructure north of Rangoon. Why were there so few railways and roads? The pamphlets in the AHB had the answers.

Burma, previously a province of British India, was a self-governing nation by the start of the war. The country stretches some 800 miles north to south and 500 miles east to west, with a tail of a further 500 miles south-eastwards down the coast bordering Siam, now Thailand. It is ringed on three sides by mountain ranges, covered in mostly primary jungle. Only to the south is the country in any way accessible, from the Bay of Bengal and the Gulf of Martaban. Three major rivers, the Salween, Sittang and Irrawaddy, run all the way down the country from the mountains and into this bay. These rivers, hills and jungles form a barrier between India and Southern China. Burma's politics, foreign relations, economy and culture had been dominated by this geography.

On the delta of the biggest river, the Irrawaddy, sits Rangoon, its Burmese name translating as 'the battle is over'. Up to the Second World War, every invader who had taken Rangoon had won the country but no successful assault had ever been mounted over the mountains from the north. Burma's geographical remoteness had led to isolationism in foreign affairs and, until they were invaded, few among the population of 17 million had had contact with, or even much knowledge of, Japan.

The economy was mostly rural, but with extensive teak forests and rubber plantations. There was oil in the central zone where, in 1941, the fields in Yenangyaung produced 250 million gallons a year. Elsewhere, considerable quantities of the rare and vital mineral wolfram, also known as tungsten, were mined. These raw materials were of great value to the Japanese, but so too, was the rice – the climate was such that two high-quality crops could be harvested each year. The majority of the Burmese in the central lowlands were hostile to British rule, and resentful of the Chinese and Indian immigrants brought in to run the oil fields and the civil bureaucracy. By 1942, there were acute ethnic tensions. The tribes of the jungles and mountains – Nagas, Karens, Shans, Kachins and Chins – were generally sympathetic to the British and met with persecution from the lowlands, where a putative Burmese National Army was waiting to welcome the Japanese.

To Europeans, the climate in Burma appears totally unforgiving. The hottest period is March to April, when the temperature in the arid central plain around Mandalay and Meiktila can climb to 100 degrees Fahrenheit at midday. In that pre-monsoon season violent westerly winds blow and unmetalled roads, paddy fields and dirt airstrips turn to clouds of choking dust. Then, no later than May, massive clouds roar in over the Bay of Bengal to dump their load over the Burmese hills as torrential rain – for some six months until October. In the Arakan Yomas, the 3,000 foot coastal range of mountains where George Hufflett first marched to meet the enemy, 200 inches fall every year. Charapunge, to the north in Indian Assam, is the wettest place on earth. In the path of the same monsoon, it gets a staggering 500 inches a year. Manchester gets just thirty-two.

All that explains why, in 1942, there were few roads and railways north of Rangoon, and none above the central plain. For both sides in the campaign, the LOC largely followed the country's rivers. They provided the main form of transport, and where there was a railway or a narrow road it ran alongside. Westwards to Indian Assam, there were merely tracks, save where a dirt road wound through the mountains to Imphal.

So that was what the poor bloody infantry and airmen were faced with – preparing to defend Burma from the much feared Japanese.

The advance on Rangoon was opposed by a thin British garrison (the bulk of British forces being trapped in Malaya) and by mid-February the invaders had reached the Sittang River, fifty miles east of the capital. A harrowing decision was taken by the commander of the British-Indian 17th Division to dynamite the bridge to deny it to the Japanese, abandoning two brigades on the enemy side. Only 3,000 made it over the river. That action, and a valiant air battle fought by the RAF and the colourful American Volunteer Group – the Flying Tigers – delayed the Japanese for two vital weeks. This allowed the 150 tanks of 7 Armoured Brigade, the 'Desert Rats', to be offloaded in Rangoon docks in the nick of time. But Rangoon was evacuated on 7 March, leaving the defenders to struggle some 600 miles north to India.

They had to fight all the way. The British/Indian divisions depended on wheeled and tracked vehicles for their movement. The enemy demonstrated much greater mobility and were able to outflank them, set up roadblocks, and pick them off. Without the tanks of 7 Armoured Brigade to break those roadblocks, retreat would have been all but impossible.

A pitifully small force of two dozen Allied aircraft did its best to support the army but to no avail. The Japanese Army Air Force had close on 300 aircraft available, brought forward to captured airstrips, and attacks on bases at Magwe and Akyab led to the RAF and the Flying Tigers ceasing to exist in Burma by the end of March.

Japanese reinforcements and supplies now poured in through Rangoon – early in April a convoy of forty ships carried an average of 5,000 tons each. Myitkyina, some 580 miles to the north, fell as early as 20 May. Then the monsoon broke and the roads, paddy fields and hastily built dirt airstrips became expanses of clinging mud.

Fighting on the eastern borders of Burma had been the 55th Chinese Division, under the command of the American General 'Vinegar Joe' Stilwell, who acted as Chief of Staff to Marshal Chiang Kai-shek, the generalissimo of the Nationalist Chinese forces. Brought from Yunnan down the Burma Road, the Chinese 200th Division had mounted a fierce defence of Toungoo, which bought the British/Indian divisions ten days of vital time to regroup. But after disaster had fallen on the Chinese on the Upper Sittang, within ten days the invaders covered 300 miles and took the town of Lashio and its railhead. The Burma Road was cut.

For the defending commanders it was now just a matter of getting their troops out of Burma. Following intense hardships and desperate heroics, 12,000 men, all under arms, struggled through the jungle and over the mountains into India, leaving '…the land of a million pagodas burning'.

Of the troops who did make it to India, and who immediately turned round and took their posts to defend the border, 10,000 were sick. They had marched through some of the most heavily malaria-infested areas in the world, and from mid-May as the monsoon rains fell, floodwaters carried infection and dysentery became endemic. In front of and behind the soldiers an estimated 400,000 Indian and Burmese refugees straggled over the border, with another 10,000 dying through disease, starvation, exposure and the guerrilla attacks of the Burmese National Army.

The Japanese advance reached the Chindwin River (a tributary of the Irrawaddy, and a mighty river in its own right), to the east of the 7,500 foot Chin Hills and less than 100 miles short of the Indian frontier. There lengthening lines of supply, and the monsoon rains, halted the enemy surge. But Burma was theirs.

At 900 miles, it had been the longest retreat in British military history. In his book *Defeat into Victory*, 'Bill' Slim, at the time lieutenant general, and commander of the British Burma Corps, wrote: 'We had taken a thorough beating. We, the Allies, had been outmanoeuvred, outfought, and outgeneralled.'

Many lessons were learnt. No doubt the speed of the Japanese advance had taken the defenders by surprise. The army garrisons, and the naval and air bases in Assam and Burma were under resourced, not least because the priorities of the Chiefs of Staff were in the Atlantic and North Africa. On the naval front, even if there had been ships and sailors to reinforce the Far East, with the Mediterranean route out of commission it would have taken all of three months for a British fleet to reach the eastern Indian Ocean round the Cape. Airfields were badly located – over on the Siam border – and open to attack. RAF squadrons were few, and their aircraft mostly obsolescent – the Japanese had, by mid-March, 260 aircraft operational against them.

One of the most valuable insights arising out of the disaster was the potential of air supply. Having on the retreat been tied to what roads there were and been given a bloody nose, General Slim saw for himself the importance of setting his soldiers free from that dependence. Later, in reporting on his plans for counterattack and liberation, he said: 'Most of us recognised that air transport could solve some of our worst problems.'

Here was a story to be told – a major and critical campaign of the Second World War, with air supply a key feature in the strategy of the British Army Commander.

Chapter 4

31 Squadron RAF

In the retreat, there were scarcely any Allied transport aircraft in the theatre capable of air supply. But there were a few, the Douglas transports of 31 Squadron RAF.

From its founding in 1915, the squadron was earmarked for service in India and took the motto *In Caelum Indicum Primus*, 'First in India Skies'. At the outbreak of the Second World War, the aircrews were flying Vickers Valentias, designated rather strangely as 'bomber transports' – the discomfort of passengers must have been acute. After patrols on the North-West Frontier, and ferrying missions to Singapore and Rangoon, there was a spell of action in 1941 in Iraq, flying troops in from India to counter the aggression of Rashid Ali. In April 1941, 'A' Flight converted to four Douglas DC-2Ks, requisitioned from Indian Airways. These, the first transports in the RAF's Indian Command, were in action from Shaibah and then Basra. One was lost at Habbaniya in a Luftwaffe Messerschmitt attack from Mosul. After further adventures in the Middle East and the Canal Zone, 31 Squadron moved to Lahore in September 1941, three months before the Japanese invasion of Burma.

A lone shuttle service was mounted between Calcutta and Rangoon until the port fell to the Japanese and then, as the Allies fought their way north across the Burmese plains, from Akyab Island on the Burmese coast to Magwe, 300 miles up the Irrawaddy from Rangoon. At the end of March 1942 the Japanese advance forced the squadron to retreat to Dum Dum airbase near Calcutta. Its battle worn DC-2s were flown to the limits, dropping supplies and medicines to retreating civilian refugees as well as to the columns of troops. They carried reinforcements and freight as far as Shwebo above Mandalay, and to Myitkyina, the vital airfield and base close to the Chinese border to the east. On return trips the aircrews brought out as many battle casualties – and, if room, refugees – as they could cram into the creaking airframes. The DC-2s were practically falling apart by then and in any other circumstances would have been grounded. The ground crews worked all hours and in all weathers to keep them airborne. The delivery of three of the more powerful and serviceable DC-3s in April was a godsend – in reality they were donated by American businessmen.

In May, now with six DC-3s, and at a new base at Dinjan, over the border in northern Assam by the Brahmaputra river, the aircrew flew sortie after sortie in the monsoon, down the mountain river valleys that were the main escape routes for the evacuation. The Japanese had now surrounded Myitkyina and on 6 May, when two DC-3s landed there, they were attacked by Japanese dive-bombers, killing two women passengers and a child. As the refugees clambered from the stricken aircraft they returned and strafed the survivors with machine guns. On the 8th, two more DC-3s were destroyed by dive-bombers while loading refugees and casualties. At dusk, Flight Lieutenant Howell and his crew landed in another DC-3 and evacuated not only the crews of the first two but also an astonishing sixty-five refugees and walking wounded – this in an aircraft designed to carry a maximum of twenty-four passengers. The next day, the airfield was captured.

From all parts of Burma, but mostly from Myitkyina, over 8,500 men, women and children were brought out by air, 4,000 of whom were carried in 31 Squadron transports. Most of the others were brought out by the US Army Air Force (USAAF), in B-17 bombers pressed into service as uncomfortable passenger aircraft, and ten Douglas C-47s diverted from Africa.

To make up for the shortage of aircraft, the aircrews of 31 Squadron were flying at times five sorties a day, over the mountains and in monsoon storms. Once, a DC-3 was seen to fly into a thundercloud, only to be ejected back the way it came, upside down. Once in May and again in June, Squadron Leader Mackie managed to land his DC-3 in a paddy field to evacuate army and civilian personnel.

Through the trials of the retreat, the squadron flew supply drops to Fort Hertz, a British base 150 miles east of Dinjan, over the Burma border and surrounded by the enemy. These deliveries of vital resources, noted by Bill Slim as the first targeted use of air supply in the campaign, ensured the fort's airstrip remained in British hands. It was to provide a vital refuelling and emergency landing ground for aircraft on the 'Hump' flights.

It was the need to supply China, their Pacific Ring ally, that was the reason for America's presence in Burma – they were certainly not there to protect European colonial interests. When the Japanese cut the Burma Road by taking Lashio there was only one option – to supply the Nationalists by air. In April 1942, Lieutenant Colonel William 'Bill' Old of the USAAF, pioneered a route to China from the airfields of northern Assam, over the lower Himalayas – the Hump. During the first summer of its operation, 13,000 Chinese troops were flown back over the mountains, for training under Stilwell in Assam, in twenty-four C-47 aircraft. This was the military version of the DC-3, the RAF and Commonwealth Air Forces giving their machines the name 'Dakota'.

The Dakotas of 31 Squadron regularly supported their American allies on the Hump operation – in the list of RAF pilots to make the trip was the name of the then officer commanding 'B' Flight, Squadron Leader Peter Bray.

In a copy of *Star News*, the magazine of the 31 Squadron RAF Association – the 'Gold Stars' – is the name and telephone number of that same Peter Bray. How much of his story might he be prepared to share? One phone call later an appointment was made to meet him at his home in Sussex. So began a rare and instructive chapter of investigation.

Chapter 5

Air Supply Pilot

On a late summer day, in the sky above Shoreham Airport a trio of Second World War fighters is practising for the air show – an auspicious introduction for this first meeting with a Burma veteran of the Royal Air Force.

There are a good number of retirement developments in Shoreham. I find the one I am looking for and press the buzzer on the security panel. The voice that answers is unmistakably officer class of an earlier generation. The door is opened and Peter Bray, lean and distinguished, comes along the carpeted corridor. He is welcoming, yet a little wary. I am, after all, a stranger looking to uncover memories that might prove painful. In their ground floor apartment he introduces his wife, Phyllis, and offers tea.

I am aware that many Second World War veterans are careful about discussing their wartime experiences. They had, after all, signed the Official Secrets Act and were forbidden for years to talk about what they were doing – it was hammered home that 'loose talk costs lives'. Also, early in the conversation, it becomes apparent that Peter, after his RAF service, had a long career as a British Airways captain, and the 1940s are a distant era. In the event, once plans have been outlined and bona fides established, he offers to help in any way he can – and gets to his feet.

'I'll go and find my log books.'

So how did he, like George Hufflett, come to find himself 5,000 miles from England, fighting the Japanese? Their early years, it turns out, could hardly have been more different.

Born in 1919 – that puts him in his eighty-eighth year – Peter's parentage was far from ordinary:

'My family on my mother's side were German, name of Lessner, but her grandfather, an engineer, took the family off to St Petersburg, in Tsarist Russia, where they founded a factory in 1853. They developed that into the area's largest, manufacturing railway locomotives, fire engines and torpedoes. It seems the company also collaborated with the Swedish Nobel armaments factory in St Petersburg, building submarines.'

He lays a one page outline of the Lessner family tree on the table, showing connections by marriage with Berlin, Dresden and Weimar:

'My paternal great-grandfather was also an engineer. He built some of the earliest tractors in England – one of them was the very first motorised vehicle to reach Australia. Then, in 1867, he too took his family, and his tractors to Russia.'

Sadly, his health didn't stand up to the harsh Russian winters and, back in England eight years later, he died leaving his wife with six children to bring up. One of them, Peter's grandfather, returned to St Petersburg, first as tutor to the children of Prince Belosselsky, and then becoming his estate manager:

'My father started work there in an insurance office and met Margit Lessner at the tennis club. They married in 1916, and that of course was just before the Revolution, so they were forced to escape through Finland and Sweden to Norway. From there it was over the North Sea from Bergen to England. My brother was one year old in that adventure. The family never returned to Russia.'

Peter was born two years later, into what was still an international family. On the Lessner side there were continuing links with Russia, and with Paris, where his grandfather Gustav lived and worked until 1930:

'Grandfather had built himself a second house in Weimar, in Germany. Every summer holiday from the age of six, I used to visit him there and got to know him very well indeed.'

That, we agree, was a pretty unusual family history, to say the least, for a young British Air Force pilot to carry into the Second World War.

Brought up in Southfields, south London, he attended Wandsworth County School, and then went into banking. In 1939, aged twenty, he was working in Barclays in the City:

'The war clouds were gathering and a pal and I decided we should do something about volunteering for the services. We thought first about the Navy, but it appeared that the Senior Service weren't falling over themselves to welcome us two lads into their wardrooms just then, so we applied to the RAF.'

Peter went for interview at Adastral House in March 1939 and was accepted for service on one of the last short entry commissions. He was instructed to report on 14 August, just a couple of weeks before the declaration of war, to London Air Park, Hanworth, for *ab initio* training:

'There was no aptitude testing. You just started flying – on the Blackburn B2 and later on the Miles Magister – and if you could do it, you were the right stuff. There were, by the way, many more flying training accidents in those days.'

He turned out to be the right stuff and completed sixty-three hours flying, thirty-two dual and thirty-one solo. After ground instruction at Initial Training Wing (ITW) and multi-engine training on Ansons at Hullavington, Acting Pilot Officer Bray was awarded his wings:

'There was a large intake of RAF aircrew trainees as the war effort built up, and an urgent need for flying instructors. I was detailed for Central Flying School – CFS – at Upavon for instructor training on the Airspeed Oxford and the Avro Tutor.'

Passing out in July 1940 as a QFI, he was posted to EFTS Ansty, near Coventry, as an instructor on Tiger Moths. After eighteen months, the demand for bomber aircrews saw him among a group of instructors sent, in March 1942, for a multi-engine refresher course at South Cerney:

> 'It was an escape from the devastation in Coventry, and we didn't see much bombing in Gloucestershire, but I remember the odd enemy plane flying across. One rather gung-ho flight commander took out his pistol and took a pot shot at one of them. He missed.'

Peter and Phyllis met at a dance in Cirencester, but the lottery of wartime postings sent him straight away to Holme-on-Spalding Moor for instrument flying training. Back in the Cotswolds, at Moreton-in-Marsh, he joined a conversion course on the twin engined medium bomber, the Vickers Wellington – known to its crews as the 'Wimpy', after the J. Wellington Wimpy character from the Popeye cartoons:

> 'I'd cycle from Moreton to Cirencester to see Phyllis – nearly thirty miles. It used to take me three hours. It was a very hilly road.'

He was then moved to Hampstead Norris, converting new pilots to the Wimpy, before receiving notice of posting overseas, to India. In July 1942 Flying Officer Bray took his leave of Phyllis (both vowing to marry on his return) to set course in a Wellington for Gibraltar, and onwards to the Gambia for the trans-Africa route:

> 'The strength of the wind took us by surprise – it was probably a jet stream, but we didn't know about them in those days. And, for security, contact with land-based stations for bearings was restricted. So we strayed well off course.
>
> 'We finally picked up a beacon on the African coast, but were still way out over the Atlantic, with the fuel gauges showing empty. In the rain and mist we were lucky to spot some sort of motorboat flying the white ensign. I told the rear gunner to shout out when he lost sight of it – he did that soon enough. The coast was still nowhere to be seen so we turned about and found the boat again. I managed to ditch

the Wimpy alongside – it floated pretty well – and we all made it.'

After finding his way back to England from West Africa, Peter and Phyllis were married rather earlier than expected, on the last day of August, with Tom Baptie, Peter's navigator, as best man. The honeymoon was in Babbacombe Bay near Torquay, where troop after troop of soldiers were under training for the North Africa campaigns. Adds Phyllis:

'I remember them marching through the streets with their tin mugs rattling against their bayonets. One night a couple of months later Peter flew off on a bombing raid on Bremen – over his grandfather's country. He met me at Newbury station the next morning, looking pretty rough.'

In November, on his twenty-third birthday, newly promoted Flight Lieutenant Bray and his crew picked up a brand new Wellington and set course again for India.

'I didn't see him for two and-a-half years,' says Phyllis quietly.

This trip too, was a catalogue of mishaps. After Gibraltar they followed a different route through North Africa but in Cairo, the Wimpy was commandeered by an operational squadron and they had to continue in a clapped out machine. Mechanical problems with that led to a forced landing in Iraq and it took two weeks to patch up the aircraft and continue. Then, out of Karachi an engine failed, causing another emergency landing and a further week's delay. Taking off again, oil loss forced a landing, on a 600 yard strip, at Udaipur in north-west India:

'They sent an engineer from Allahabad but, of course, at 600 yards the strip was not long enough for the Wimpy to take off. Contractors had to be brought in to lengthen the runway to 1,000 yards – it took about a month. But we didn't complain – we spent Christmas in a luxurious guesthouse in Udaipur. I remember the local Maharajah visiting us and sitting in the Wellington cockpit. In return he invited us to visit his palace and we had a great time riding on his elephants.

'We made it back to Karachi where the Wimpy was

promptly sent to a maintenance unit and written off. After all that effort, I found myself on a ferrying unit, flying Vengeances, Hurricanes and Blenheims to the action over in the east. But it was only for a few weeks.'

In March, he and his whole Wellington crew, including the bomb aimer and rear gunner, arrived in Dhubalia, Bengal, to join Wing Commander Bill Burbury's 31 Squadron on air supply duties. They found their new colleagues busy flying sorties in support of the First Chindit Expedition.

Chapter 6

Bully and Bullets to the Chindits

The shelves at Bentley Priory are a rich source of Chindit stories. In England, the so-called 'forgotten' war in Burma generally took second place in the public mind to the momentous events nearer home, but the Chindits, with their marauding long range adventures behind Japanese lines, were a certainty to hit the headlines. What was their place in the campaign, and how did they use air supply?

Following the Japanese exertions in their headlong advance through Burma in 1942 and the Allies' sufferings on their retreat, both sides accepted the onset of the monsoon in May as a chance to lick their wounds and consolidate their positions.

The enemy sat behind the Chindwin river while they brought in reinforcements, and built up their airfields and bases across Burma for a planned attack on India. Britain and the USA were fully stretched in other theatres and in any event hadn't the base facilities in India for mounting offensive operations – almost all their effort was aimed at creating such facilities. The main aim of the Americans was to build the infrastructure to support the Hump operation, and to prepare for an advance southwards from Ledo to link up with the Burma Road. The British wanted to defend India and construct a springboard to liberate the lost Burmese territories and this needed a massive reorientation from the North-West Frontier, the pre-war focus, to Bengal and Assam in the east.

None of these war aims could be feasible without superiority in the air. In 1942, the Japanese Army Air Force (JAAF) had the aeroplanes to give them almost full command of the skies. But with only fifteen operational airfields in Burma and with the monsoon raging, the squadrons were withdrawn to southern Burma, Malaya and Singapore for refurbishment and retraining in preparation for the planned post monsoon invasion of India. The aircraft numbered fifty Mitsubishi heavy bombers (codenamed 'Sally' by the Allies), seven Kawasaki 'Lily' light bombers, fourteen Mitsubishi 'Dinahs' for high level reconnaissance, and about 100 Nakajima 'Oscar' single engined fighters.

The Dinah, with a service ceiling of 34,000 feet and a range of 1,540 miles, flew unthreatened by the RAF and USAAF fighters in the theatre in 1942 and a large part of 1943. The Oscar was a land based development of the Japanese navy's formidable 'Zero', and with its maximum speed of just over 300 miles per hour, outstanding manoeuvrability and battle-trained and determined pilots, it was an elusive target for the Allies. But its weakness was its lack of armour and self-sealing fuel tanks. The RAF's Hurricane fighter pilots, repelling Japanese attacks on Colombo and Trincomalee in April, worked out that by gaining height and diving at speed, they could catch the Oscars napping and blow them up with machine-gun fire.

However, when Burma fell, there were few Hurricanes remaining. To rebuild Allied air power, everything had to start from scratch, and Burma was bottom of the priority list for men, materials and equipment. With the disaster at Tobruk in June, shipments, and transport and fighter aircraft were diverted from India to North Africa. For bombers the priority was attacking German cities. Nevertheless, throughout the retreat and despite the 1942 monsoon, the Sappers had continued the construction of more than 200 airstrips in Assam. Eventually men, support engineering, fuel, and radar units for these bases began to arrive, together with aircraft.

For the RAF came the Wellington medium bombers which were being replaced by the Lancaster in Europe, and by October there were two squadrons at Jessore. US built Vultee Vengeance dive-bombers started to fly in, together with older marks of the Spitfire from Europe. In November they were joined by Bristol Beaufighters for reconnaissance. By the end of the year the Sappers, and thousands of local labourers, had built 148 new strips, eighty-three with all-weather runways. The RAF Air

Commander, Air Chief Marshal Sir Richard Peirse, had his forces in much better shape for countering the expected Japanese air offensive.

This build-up of air power had to dovetail with the needs of the army. While the Allied Divisional Commanders were reinforcing the combat power of their units, they ordered regular forward patrols. Although no more than a series of minor offensives, these gave the soldiers a baptism of contact with the feared Japanese, in which they learnt that they were an enemy that could be beaten in close combat.

At the same time, the efforts of the Sappers and miners of the 7th Indian Division restored the vital road from Manipur, the Assam railhead, to Imphal, the main Allied army and air base in the hills bordering Burma. They managed this by Christmas 1943, enabling supplies to be brought overland to strengthen garrisons, squadrons and field hospitals in the face of the expected Japanese push for India.

But one major counterattack was mounted in mid-December 1942 by the 14th Indian Division in the Arakan (an 'Indian Division' in the British Army comprised two brigades from the Indian Army together with one from the British). With reinforcement from the 2nd British Division, the attack lasted until March 1943. However, after sustaining 2,500 casualties (with many more incapacitated by malaria and other diseases) the Allies were back where they started. But the RAF flew some 2,000 sorties during this campaign, the four fighter squadrons often putting up 150 sorties in a day, the performance of the Spitfires against the Oscars crucial in beating back Japanese air power. This success in some way offset the reverses on the ground.

The Allied commanders took lessons from that failed offensive. Their troops had heard terrifying reports of Japanese atrocities, that prisoners were tortured, even the wounded. As a result, the soldiers brought their injured comrades back with them, slowing their retreat with often fatal consequences. Then, the usual Japanese tactic was to encircle Allied forces, who were dependent on wheeled transport, throw up roadblocks and cut off their retreat. It was realised that, re-supplied by air, they could stand their ground. In addition, where the aircraft could land, the wounded could be flown out.

The Allied staff officers could now see the importance of the air transport, not only for positioning airborne and parachute forces, but also for air supply. Without the latter, all rations, fuel and ammunition would have to be moved by road, under constant threat of ambush. They would then have to be carried into the jungle by the troops themselves, slowing them down and limiting their time on patrol and penetration. As a result, an Anglo-American Troop Carrier Command was set up, under the American Brigadier General William Old, tasked with delivering cargoes at the rate of 10,000 tons a month for the planned 1943 spring offensive.

But air supply, in slow, unarmed transport aircraft, flying at low level for air drop, would be impossible without air superiority. That was the task of the fighters and bombers.

The Allied air forces now went on the offensive, RAF bombers taking on targets within a radius of 250 miles and those of the newly arrived B-24 Liberators of the USAAF attacking farther afield. The Japanese air forces were driven back from the frontline along the Chindwin. The skies, although not free of Japanese fighters, were safe enough for the initial test of the new air supply organisation – supporting the First Chindit Expedition.

Throughout 1942, General Stilwell had been consolidating his American and Chinese forces in the north of Assam, and an advance was planned for them into Burma in March, from the Yunnan province in China. The Chindit guerrilla fighters, led by the charismatic Brigadier Orde Wingate, were to cross the Chindwin and march 200 miles behind Japanese lines, to cause havoc with enemy supply and communications. In the event, mainly through the machinations of Chiang Kai-shek, the Chinese advance was cancelled. Nevertheless the Allied commanders decided that the Wingate expedition should go ahead.

Wingate himself chose to name his troops the 'Chindits' after a fabulous Burmese animal, whose effigy guarded many a temple. They were British Army infantrymen – all, in the words of the Commander-in-Chief, General Sir Archibald Wavell, 'men of ordinary line battalions, sent originally to India for garrison duty, not specially picked daredevils'. The majority were townsmen, who had been in Liverpool, Manchester and Birmingham just a year before.

Seven columns with about 400 men in each, moved off on foot from Imphal on 7 February 1943. As a decoy, a couple of columns of Gurkhas crossed the Chindwin three days ahead of the main body and fifty miles to the south. The brigade strength force was to cover some 750 to 1,000 miles before the end of April. They took with them hundreds of pack mules, oxen and even elephants, but the RAF was to be their main supply line. To avoid the risks to their vulnerable jungle LOC, the goods were to arrive, in Wingate's words, 'like Father Christmas, down the chimney'.

There was a senior RAF officer on Wingate's staff with an RAF liaison officer, and two wireless operators marching with each column. They worked directly with the column commanders, advising on locations for the dropping zones (DZs) and calling in the air drop aircraft. These were the DC-3s of 31 Squadron, supported for the first time by 194 Squadron. This squadron, formed the previous year from 31's 'C' Flight, was operating out of Tezpur with the Lockheed Hudson, an American-built light bomber and coastal reconnaissance aircraft. It was not ideal for supply dropping, but the aircrews did the job.

The airmen were learning the art of the air drop as they went along, and in the expedition's early stages an average of one in ten packs was lost. But there was plenty of opportunity for practice. For instance, a mammoth drop at Tonmakeng to Brigade Headquarters and the five columns attached to it, took three days to complete. On 12 March, with a few weeks' experience under their belts, all the chutes in a supply drop at Pegon were reported by the RAF liaison officer to be 'beautifully and symmetrically in middle of the paddy'.

On that occasion the delivery consisted of five days' rations, petrol, mail, newspapers and paperback books – but no boots and clothing of which the soldiers were in dire need. Another column got a supply drop they didn't indent for. Some drops were made 'on spec', the original planned schedule being honoured without confirmation from the receiving column. This showed the difficulties of communication, which became even more acute as the Chindits crossed the Irrawaddy and, harassed by the enemy, were forced to move away from the notified DZ before the aircraft arrived with the load. The DZs were often no more than 10 yard-square holes in the jungle and to guide the aircrews in, ground signals were deployed by day, and lights used at night. But the Japanese set out decoys to lure the aircraft away, or worse still, set up an ambush around the site of a drop.

Shortages of aircraft led to difficulties. One column was desperate for rations but the aircraft failed to take-off because of engine failure, and there was no back up. Finding the exact spot for the DZ was difficult both from the air and on the ground. A column RAF liaison officer reported that the supply aircraft could be heard circling no more than a mile away, but the packs took three patrols two hours to find. It was not easy to march onto a sound in the jungle.

That drop included bully beef (canned corned beef) which had not been seen for weeks. The standard five-day ration, which was originally designed for paratroops, contained twelve hardtack biscuits, 2ozs of cheese, nuts and raisins, dates, twenty cigarettes, tea, sugar, dried milk, acid drops or chocolate, and a packet of salt – total weight 2lbs. Other consignments included boots, shirts, socks and trousers – these being perishable items in the heat and humidity. One column was surprised to be showered with silver rupees from a ruptured pack. A note followed them down saying: Enclosed Please Find 5,000 Rupees – the soldiers reportedly tracked down around 3,000 of them.

Personnel were parachuted in from time to time. Two sig-nallers were dropped into a DZ with Japanese in the undergrowth on one side and the British on the other. Both sides waved them over and mercifully, they worked out which ones were the enemy.

Without air supply the expedition could never have been mounted, and to date it was the most successful example of army and air force close cooperation. But the men on the ground were forced by Japanese attacks and sheer exhaustion to split up into smaller parties which set out to make their way back to India as best they could. Wireless sets and signallers were lost, and air supply aircraft could no longer find the men to make the drop.

Five-day ration packs had to be eked out for as long as three weeks. Boots fell to pieces – many were marching in tattered rubber shoes meant only for river crossings – and feet were never dry. Foot rot made them too painful to touch. Craving sugar, men resorted to chewing green fruit, boiled grass and poisonous bitter red berries. A lucky few survived on a couple of malted milk tablets a day. Dozens drowned in the fast-flowing rivers. Some turned up in China and some at Fort Hertz, having walked over 100 miles in mountainous jungle in six days. Just 65 per cent of those who set out in February made it back alive.

It was admitted in the reports that the First Chindit Expedition achieved very little that was tangible. They blew up bits of a railway, which did not take long to repair, gathered some useful intelligence, distracted the Japanese from other operations and killed a few hundred of an army which numbered in the hundred thousands. But Wavell took three positives from the foray. After twelve months of Japanese occupation and propa-ganda, the Chindits had found more friends in this adventure than did the enemy. The swashbuckling of Wingate and his men behind enemy lines was proving a great boost to Allied morale, in Burma and at home. And the whole exercise had shown that it was feasible to maintain a force in the field by supply dropping alone.

It was common knowledge that Japanese troops and their Burmese collaborators murdered prisoners. Unable to move their wounded, the Chindits were forced to leave them with their packs, water, and a grenade. In this dire situation, one 31 Squadron crew achieved an outstanding feat of airmanship. On Easter Sunday, 27 April, on the retreat, a party of twenty-five men, led by Lieutenant Colonel Sam Cooke, was about the only group still in wireless contact with Imphal. Just north of the Irrawaddy, still 200 miles behind Japanese lines, they signalled that they'd found a possible landing ground in a jungle clearing.

Against all the odds, the Dakota, piloted by Flying Officer Michael Vlasto, found the spot – the men had laid out the message: 'Plane Land Here', in lengths of parachute silk – and managed an improbable landing on the makeshift strip. With the shortest of possible take-offs Vlasto contrived to miss the surrounding jungle trees and flew out seventeen sick and wounded.

In this first major air supply operation the logistics organisation was impressively effective. The team that the twenty-three year old Flight Lieutenant Peter Bray joined in March 1943 was learning on the job, but the logistics planners had put a lot of effort into getting it right first time. First, the men at base stores had to make sure that the right supplies, in the right quantities, were forwarded to the Agatarla supply dropping base. There, the men of the Royal Army and Royal Indian Army Service Corps had to break down the goods into the right parapacks and load them into the aircraft in the correct order for dropping – all this on demand, initiated by the wireless messages from the jungle columns. In issuing the flying orders and vectoring the aircrews onto the correct DZs, the operations staff had a key task.

Squadron ground crews kept the transports serviceable so that aircrews could fly them to jungle clearings on no more than a map coordinate and, flying low and slow over enemy territory, heave the stuff out, accurately, on up to a dozen runs. It worked well. In 178 sorties the Dakotas and Hudsons delivered over 500 tons of essentials to the struggling and straggling columns, and kept them in business.

Smaller drops continued at Fort Hertz, and to Chinese-American units in the Hukawng valley, remote in the north of Burma. But the main bulk of supplies in the first half of 1943 was delivered in the Naga Hills on the border north of Imphal, and in the Chin Hills to the south. Here, over the border in Burma, units of the Allied Army were occupying remote strongpoints, west of the Chindwin and not yet overwhelmed by the Japanese tide.

Haka and Tiddim were two such outposts. Both 150 miles east of Agatarla, and high in the 6,000 feet spinal ranges of the Burmese Chin Hills, they lay just twenty miles short of the

Japanese lines. By May, the monsoon was in full force but the transports kept flying. That month, Peter Bray and his crew, newly converted to the Dakota, made the first of their many supply drops at Tiddim:

> 'To find our way to the DZ, we flew at low level in the valleys, map reading. That also gave us the best chance of avoiding any Jap fighters which braved the monsoon. Trouble was, operating just above the jungle tops brought our Dakotas into range of enemy machine guns. But certainly the weather was the biggest hazard – driving wind and rain, and cloud. I wouldn't have liked to do it in anything other than the Dak.'

That rugged, willing and forgiving aeroplane was in effect the secret weapon of the Allies, making tactical air supply of an army a feasible option. How did the Dakota come to arrive on the scene just at the right time to make this revolutionary tactic possible?

Chapter 7

Dakotas Fly In

The DC transports were the brainchild of Donald Wills Douglas who, born in 1892, had established one of the first aircraft manufacturing companies in the United States. The first was designed and built in response to a requirement specification from Transcontinental & Western Air Inc, based in Kansas City. They wanted an airliner that could cross the United States and clear the Rocky Mountains. The resulting Douglas Cloudster, designed by engineers Arthur E. Raymond and James H. Kindelberger, first flew on 21 February 1921 and was an immediate success. Orders were placed for production aircraft, with the series name DC-2.

American Airlines caught the mood and proposed a stretched and wider version of the DC-2, to be called the Douglas Sleeper. This, the DC-3, had its first flight on 17 December 1935 at the Douglas factory in Santa Monica, California. It represented an outstanding advance in aircraft design. It was larger, faster and more luxurious than anything else in the air. It carried twenty-one passengers in a heated and soundproofed cabin and was the first passenger airliner with an automatic pilot and retractable hydraulic landing gear. Selling for $110,000, it could fly from New York to Chicago non-stop, and coast-to-coast in fifteen hours.

The DC-3 was powered initially by two Wright Cyclone R-1820 series 14-cylinder radial petrol, propeller-driven engines. The DC-3A came along with the more powerful Pratt & Whitney Twin Wasp R-1830 14-cylinder radial, with an initial rating in 1936 of 1,000 horsepower. This was enhanced to 1,250 three years later, and gave a maximum operating altitude of 24,300 feet, more than matching the requirement for climbing over the Rockies.

Standardisation of production parts reduced maintenance costs and helped to break all safety records. The operating cost per seat-mile of the DC-3 was one third less than for the DC-2, enabling American Airlines in 1936 to make its first ever operating profit. With the DC-3, airlines could make money out of carrying passengers – in effect Mr Douglas's venture made commercial aviation possible.

By 1939, 455 commercial models of the DC-3 were in service all around the globe, flying 90 per cent of the world's airline business. KLM of the Netherlands, the world's oldest airline, was the first overseas user. The Dutch aircraft company Fokker had a licence for assembly, and the Russians and Japanese had licences to build. By 1940, DC-3s had flown 100 million miles and carried some 3 million passengers.

Following the outbreak of war in Europe, the United States Army Air Command, despite the opposition of the isolationist lobby in the US Government, commissioned a military version of the DC-3. The specification was for an aircraft whose prime purpose was to be the movement of supplies and personnel to front-line airfields and the evacuation of the sick and wounded – air-drop capability was not a consideration at the time. The resulting C-47 more than met its design requirements and on 16 September 1940, Army Air Command ordered 545 of them, which they called the Skytrain. The US Navy ordered thirty and the production line was under way.

Under the demands of war, continuing aerofoil improvements were made and gross weight was increased to 26,000lbs. Stories circulated of its amazing ruggedness – one had managed to land after a mid-air collision in which twelve feet of wing was lost, without one rivet being loosened in the remainder of the airframe. The strength came from the box-frame rigid wing spar built into a fuselage with seven bulkhead-strengthened compartments. Freight payload increased to 7,500lbs (more than double the original specification), or twenty-eight paratroops, or fourteen stretchers for casualty evacuation (casevac) – carried at a cruising speed of 150 knots. It was a bonus that the tail wheel configuration brought the single, port side door down close enough to the ground for ungainly military freight to be loaded. It could have been custom designed for Burma.

At the end of the 1942 retreat, when Bill Slim saw the need for transport aircraft, he wrote, 'We have none of our own. They will have to come from America'. Again, he was right.

The Douglas transports first found their way into the UK when, on the fall of Holland, KLM's aircraft were flown across the North Sea and continued their service in British markings. Later, under Lend-Lease arrangements, the first RAF Dakotas were fitted with auxiliary fuel tanks in the freight cabin and ferried across the Atlantic, from Presqu'Isle in Maine to Prestwick in Scotland. The first to arrive in Assam, in April 1943, were allocated to 31 Squadron, and went into immediate action air dropping to the Chindits. In June the same year, it was the turn of 62 Squadron to convert to Dakotas.

But with more and more Dakotas coming into the Assam bases, there was a pressing need for aircrews to fly them. Were there more men like Peter Bray, ready to tell their stories of Dakota operations? Enquiries were made through an issue of 31 Squadron's magazine and within days, the telephone rang.

Chapter 8

Policeman to Pilot

It is a Sunday evening. A voice with a soft North American accent comes on the line:

'Hallo, I'm Norman Currell. I've read your piece in *Star News* and I reckon I might be able to help. I was on 31 Squadron in Burma, flying Dakotas.'

He is calling from Canada, where he has lived, he says, ever since the war:

'I came out here for RAF pilot training under the Empire Training scheme – that was in January 1942. I earned my Wings and then I guess I was lucky enough, and just about competent enough, to be made an instructor. What with one thing and another I didn't get out to Burma, to Ramree Island, until June 1945.'

Late in the campaign as that was, there would still be much to be told about his part in the air supply story:

'We had some hair-raising times over there in Burma. I've always been going to write it all down, but life and business roll on and the years go by. I'm in my nineties now and my handwriting's not so good, but I've got my old typewriter. Maybe helping with this book of yours is just what I need to get started. Shall I begin at the beginning?'

I say I'd be delighted to hear about as many of his experiences as he'd be comfortable with, and we ring off, promising to keep in touch. True to his word, a few weeks later fifty closely-typed pages of eventful autobiographical history arrive from over the Atlantic, with permission to use as I see fit.

Norman was born in Peckham, south London in January 1914:

'I was my parents' first child. My dad worked in Grindlays Bank, by the Cenotaph in Whitehall. When the Great War broke out he went to France with the Old Contemptibles and was one of the youngest sergeant majors in the British forces. He survived the trenches but the whole thing ruined his health and in 1921 we moved out to Essex for the fresher air.'

He won a scholarship to Brentwood Grammar School and, in 1931, went to work at the same Grindlay's Bank where his father had been a clerk:

'The two-hours each way on the train made for a very long day. Then, walking along the Thames Embankment I saw this good-looking ship, HMS *President*, moored at Blackfriars. It turned out to be the headquarters of the Royal Naval Volunteer Reserve – RNVR – and I went aboard to see what I could find.'

What he found was a rewarding and sociable opportunity for playing at sailors:

'Two evenings each week were spent on naval and gunnery drills. It was a joy, after work, to get out of my bank clothes and sleep in a hammock, and best of all, miss that damned commute. In the summer we had a week at a time, and would sail down to Canvey Island or row up to Teddington. It made the job at the bank just about tolerable.'

But not tolerable enough. By the beginning of 1932 the call of the sea became too strong and, with the kind assistance of Grindlay's shipping department, Norman signed papers to enlist as an Apprentice Deck Officer with Houlder Bros S.S. Line on the South America run:

'On the first day of March, aged just eighteen, I took the train to Liverpool to join *El Paraguajo*. There were four of us apprentices all crammed into one cabin. Ginger, the senior, had two trips under his belt and ruled the roost. Jock from Aberdeenshire had a Scottish brogue so thick that he was with us for at least a week before we understood a word he was saying. We were allocated four-hourly watches with the officers and four hours of working under the bosun. I was on the midnight watch with the second mate.'

El Paraguajo was a 10,000-ton twin-screw 'meat ship' which made thirteen-week round trips to Montevideo (to discharge cargo) then across the River Plate to Buenos Aires (discharging more cargo in exchange for 5,000 tons of chilled beef) before ploughing back through Atlantic storms to Liverpool:

'We had four weeks in port at Buenos Aires. On half-a-crown a week, all we apprentices could afford was the Mission to Seamen – a Church of England effort to provide some alternative to the bars, whorehouses and gambling dens downtown. To augment my pay, I went over to the boxing hall each Tuesday and Friday, where I could get one peso a fight. Once, we came back through Rio to load bananas. We sailed into harbour at eleven at night, past the Balnareo waterfront with its neon lights, with the hills all around and the Jesus Christ statue floodlit on the summit. Unforgettable.

'We did three of those roundtrips, and then, at home on my first leave I received instructions to transfer, with Jock, to one of Houlder's 5,000-ton tramp ships. The single screw *Gambia River* was a real come down. She had been laid up in Newport for at least twelve months and was in dire need of a damned good clean up. We were ten days in the rain at Swansea (the piss pot of Wales, some said), loading sheet metal for Argentina. What a trip that was. We ran into one hell of a storm in the Bay of Biscay – two days it lasted, and broke the propeller. We had to put into Lisbon to change it. Three days that took, and then, as the old gut-bucket only did nine knots with the wind behind her, it took us three weeks to reach Rosario.'

But Norman was to make a further three Atlantic crossings,

before being transferred to another 10,000-tonner on the South American run:

'On the last trip home we watched a team of sharks and swordfish ganging up against a whale. The swordfish got underneath the whale, then the largest shark reared out of the water and crashed down on the whale's head, beating him unconscious. Then they all tore him to pieces. Horrible but fascinating to watch.

'Then, a day or two before reaching Tenerife, I developed terrible pains in my abdomen – turned out to be appendicitis. As soon as we docked I was whisked off for an emergency operation, which sorted me out. My ship sailed off without me but as soon as I could get around under my own steam, I hauled myself up the gangplank of the *Africa Star*, bound for London.'

For Norman, the wheel of fortune had now spun decisively:

'It was while recuperating in rural Essex that I saw an advert for recruits to the County Constabulary. I realised it was going to take several years before I could think of getting my second mate's ticket so I applied. After testing interviews I was lucky enough to be one of the score of candidates accepted for training in Chelmsford. The ten-week course was pretty demanding – criminal law, powers of arrest, first aid, swimming and rescue from the water, traffic control, jujitsu for protecting ourselves or arresting unwilling offenders, and use of handcuffs and truncheons.

'On graduation at the beginning of 1935, I was sent to Braintree for a two-year probationary period. There was very little crime there, so it was ironic when I myself was charged with, and convicted of dangerous driving on a motorbike. I'd run into the back of a lorry, one owned by a trucking operation – always in trouble with the law, as it happened. But I still collected a five-pound fine and a twelve-month driving suspension.'

He must have acquitted himself acceptably overall however, for at the end of the two years he was posted to Hornchurch as a police constable:

'By the spring of '38 the news from Europe was not looking good. Nazi Germany was making warlike noises and had sent its air force to Spain on the side of Franco. The British Police Forces were given responsibility for training the Air Raid Warden service. I volunteered for training as instructor in high-explosive bombs, anti-gas measures and fire fighting. We gave presentations to thirty wardens for two hours at a time. Afterwards, we'd address four to five hundred citizens on self-help measures. When the Blitz started, what with the big RAF base at Hornchurch on our beat and the docks down the road, all that was put to good use, I can tell you.'

Norman was promoted to sergeant at the almost unheard of early age of twenty-six, and was transferred to Romford:

'Then, when it became quite obvious that Germany was far too occupied with its attack on Russia to give much attention to us, and the threat of invasion had long since passed, it became possible to think in aggressive terms. The authorities decided that some reserved occupations, including the police, could allow their members to join the armed forces. Officers, like me, could apply to the Fleet Air Arm or the Royal Air Force. With my prior attachment to the RNVR and my years in the Merchant Navy, my first choice was for the Fleet Air Arm. However, it seemed that with few aircraft, and fewer carriers they were in no condition to accept any new pilots, so I transferred my application to the RAF.'

In January 1942, at the Aircrew Receiving Centre at St John's Wood, candidates went through a series of examinations, mental and physical:

'I was deemed to have the necessary aptitude for training as a pilot and was posted to Torquay for initial instruction. The course lasted from 14 February to 28 May and was in the atmospheric surroundings of Rose Tor Abbey, which in a previous conflict had served to house nearly five hundred Spanish prisoners from the ill-fated Armada.

'Basic instruction consisted of a little RAF history, and a lot of rules, ranks and proper conduct. We did some elementary maths, an introduction to laying out a navigation plan, and aircraft recognition. It was really quite a pleasant holiday by the seaside. We were marched up and down the hills by a corporal who said, it was '...to strengthen the legs for possible parachute jumping'. Quite a number of commercial companies had been moved out of London – and in the evenings their female staff, and the town girls, made great company.

'Most of the sixty or so on the course were straight out of Civvy Street, although there were a few senior NCOs who seemed to look upon the whole idea of remustering to aircrew as a bit of a joke.

'There was no flying at Torquay. That was scheduled to be in Canada under the British Commonwealth Air Training Scheme. For those who couldn't cut the mustard as pilots, there were training facilities waiting for navigators, wireless operators and air gunners. But those of us who had been police officers had to make the grade as pilots or navigators – or be sent back to the Force with our tails between our legs.'

In due course LAC Currell was posted to Clydebank to take passage on the American troopship *Thomas H. Barry*, sailing in convoy with an escort of half a dozen United States Navy destroyers:

'There were hordes of us RAF types on board. There wasn't much to do – the most exciting thing was to watch the Yankee sailors losing hundreds of dollars shooting crap dice. The food on the ship was great, such as we hadn't seen since rationing was enforced at home. I remember being on kitchen fatigue one evening and having with five others to crack literally thousands of eggs for the next morning's breakfast, and on the last evening we were served up a complete half roast chicken – each.

'Landfall was in New York, but we didn't see much of that, nor of America itself. We were herded onto the train for the RCAF Personnel Depot at Moncton, New Brunswick, where we arrived on 28 June 1942. The town was so peaceful – no air-raids, blackout or rationing – and the food! Downtown, four of us ordered steaks. In came a huge platter with a slab of meat hanging over the edges, and we started to cut it into four pieces. You guessed it. In came three more – one for each of us!

'In mid-July, a group of us would-be fliers boarded a train and headed west. We were completely overwhelmed by the scale of everything. The train rumbled on, with forests opening up in front of us and then closing in behind, the whole night. In Winnipeg, a bevy of charming young ladies laid on a real party for us with some real western hospitality. All too soon, "All aboard" was heard and it was more woods, for a second night. The next day we stopped at Moose Jaw for another warm welcome.

'The final halt for a group of sixty of us was Caron, Saskatchewan. We stood with our kitbags in the late evening light, surrounded by an immensity of cornfields. The only features we could pick out were a couple of grain elevators. Shortly, three trucks drove up to take us some distance north to Number 33, Boundary Bay Elementary Flying School of the British Commonwealth Air Training Scheme.'

Accommodation for the newcomers was in large H-type huts, the standard for Other Ranks in the RCAF. They were not kept waiting long before getting into the air:

'I see from my logbook that my very first venture into the wide blue yonder occurred on 20 July – just two days after our arrival – in the venerable Tiger Moth, serial number 4070, under the instruction of one Pilot Officer Harris. It was thirty minutes of air experience, cockpit layout and effect of controls. We moved quickly to straight and level flying, medium and steep turns and stalling and spinning. There was a lot to take in but I seemed to be coping – except that I couldn't for the life of me put the thing on the ground.

'After some ten and a half hours' flying time, I was handed over to a sergeant pilot who worked on me and my landing difficulties for another two hours. It seemed I just couldn't judge my height above the ground – Lack of Depth Perception it was called. But my sergeant pilot must have brought me on enough for off I went on my own – for the first, and very nearly the last, time.

'On my first attempt at landing I bounced high in the air, shoved on the power – and did a 360 degree turn a few feet off the ground. Somehow I got back into a climb away and on my second go I got the poor old Tiger down. My instructor greeted me with, "There has to be something good to say about a landing if you can walk away from it."

'Anyhow, I'd broken the jinx and I completed the course – rated average – on 5 September, with seventy-seven hours' flying, of which forty were solo by day and a couple at night. I shudder now to think that in World War One, pilots with that amount of experience were said to be ready for frontline duty.'

The next stage of the course was at Carberry, Manitoba on the twin-engined Avro Anson:

'On my first night solo I again came close to oblivion when I lost sight of the gooseneck flares and came in too low on the approach. I was shocked to see telephone wires going over my head! I opened the throttles wide, bounced through the top wire of the perimeter fence and just made it to the runway. I learned a lot about controlling the height on approach that night.'

With the end of the course approaching Norman and his mates were all anxious to know what postings they would get:

'We all thought we were destined to be bomber pilots. Someone got a peek at the sheet of names showing our postings and everyone was going that route – except for me. I was astounded to find that I was slated to go to Number 2 Flying Instructors School. I wasn't best pleased to be singled out from my mates and went straight to the bosses to remonstrate. To my amazement they said, "You've had police experience and you're just the type we're looking for."

'I can see now that it was probably a lifesaver for me. Had I gone back to the UK, I would have been ready to join a bomber squadron by the Fall of '43 and, as we all know, the chances of completing even one tour of duty on bombers were odds very much against.'

As it was, Pilot Officer Currell, sporting his new wings moved on to Vulcan, Calgary. In March 1943, with 300 hours in his logbook, he graduated as a Qualified Flying Instructor. He was to have completed some 1,500 hours in Canada before in May 1945, as a thirty year old flying officer he was posted to the Long Range Operational Training Unit at Comox for conversion to the Dakota. He was on course to replace Peter Bray as a captain on 31 Squadron.

Chapter 9

British Raj to Burma

A telephone call from his wife, Jean was the first contact with Colin Lynch. She said that they had seen the piece in *Star News* and that her husband had thought about responding. He had been an aircrew observer in Burma on 31 Squadron Dakotas but he had kept pretty quiet over the years about his experiences out there. He had, however, agreed to her making an exploratory call, at the end of which, he was prepared to arrange a meeting.

In the living room of their cosy bungalow in Hillingdon, north of Heathrow airport, it becomes clear that Colin could offer an account full of incident and variety. The walls are covered with many of his paintings – evidence of a long and successful post-war career as a graphic designer and artist. There are also pictures of him with his crew and their Dakota on air supply in Burma. A tall man, with a ready wit, and a lilting Irish colonial accent, he is soon in full flow.

Before being pitch-forked into the cauldron of Burma, he'd already had a series of encounters with the finger of fate:

> 'I was born in August 1922 in Rawalpindi. There were eight of us, but three died young in enteric fever epidemics. That was one of the health hazards in those days. My great-grandfather was the first of the Lynches to leave Ireland – he travelled by stages to the Far East. He and his family were in Malacca when my grandfather took off for India and got a job as an official in the North-West Railway Company. My father followed him into the company.'

Colin's father Hugh rose to a high rank, well versed in railway administration, engineering and law, and his mother was the orphan of a British couple. She and Hugh began their married life by adopting the five orphaned children of an Anglo-Portuguese family and went on to adopt four more orphans. With the eight of their own that meant a total of seventeen children – and two sittings at table when they were all at home:

'My father was stationed in various places but then we settled in Delhi. In our house – a lovely big colonial bungalow – we had all kinds of servants. I remember a cook, a bearer who waited at table, a sweeper, two gardeners, a chauffeur, a chaprassi or messenger, an ayah for the children – and a Muslim tailor. He worked on our verandah, running up everything we wanted on his sewing machine.

'We enjoyed many social and sporting activities. Game hunting and fishing were very popular – my parents made sure that all of us boys upheld the highest code of conduct in these activities, including the correct preparation of game and fowl for the kitchen table.

'My mother and sister had gained their LRAMs on the piano. My mother gave concerts and with my sisters playing piano and violin, musical soirées were frequent events at home and at friends' houses. I used to butt in with my harmonica and ukulele playing!'

He admits that, as the youngest of four boys, he was his mother's favourite and somewhat spoilt. But he was also a bit of a rascal:

'With my brother, Vic, I got into a lot of scrapes. We decided we needed a play pit in the garden, and chose a spot right alongside two Moghul graves. The servants said we shouldn't as it was sacred ground – but we did, and sure enough, we both went down with a high fever. The servants said we were cursed by the graves and wouldn't get better until the pit was filled in. So it was – and we recovered. We decided they were probably right about the curse and gave those graves a wide berth from then on.

'My father used to go on inspection tours of the North-

West Railway. The family sometimes accompanied him in his private carriage and there were several occasions when we met and dined with tribal leaders who were loyal to the Crown. There were some hairy experiences! On one journey through the Khyber Pass, rebels ambushed our train, and shot and killed the driver. The army stationed nearby drove them off, a new driver was put on the engine and we proceeded on our journey.

'About a year later, I was bitten by a bull terrier which came running up our garden path. I thought it was ours and it was only when my sister and the ayah jumped onto the kitchen table that I realised its behaviour was more than strange. It cornered me and bit me – fourteen times, here on my legs. You can still see the scars. Medics arrived and took me off to the local hospital. The dog had been shot and when its brain was removed for analysis, they found it was rabid. My wounds were cauterised and they gave me an anti-rabies injection in the stomach. I was then taken to the Pasteur Institute for the full course. It was a two day journey by train to the only institute that specialised in this treatment and it was right up in the hills! My mother was warned that my chances of recovery were slim – but against all the odds, after three months' observation, I was declared out of danger. My recovery after being bitten by a rabid dog made medical history and was headlined in the press of the day.

Those escapades gave Colin a matter-of-fact attitude to death, which, given the high mortality rate from disease, he shared with most of the inhabitants of British India.

In the Naini Tal hill-station, United Provinces, 7,600 feet up in the Himalayan mountains, there were eight boarding schools. All the boys and girls born to Mr and Mrs Lynch went to one or another of them and, in 1929, at the tender age of six and a half, Colin started at All Saints' School, where he attended the Higher Kindergarten. The school was co-ed and run by nuns – sticklers for discipline. He arrived there in March, for nine long months, after which he was ready for his next school, where the regime was even stricter:

Sherwood College was a boys' school, run on the lines of Eton and Harrow. Its motto was *Mereat Quisque Palmam*, meaning: Let Each Deserve a Prize. Vic was three years ahead of me, and we were both taken to school on the railway by my parents. It was a long 150 miles to the end of the line. There, we were sometimes taken by car and sometimes packed into a bus to zigzag up the hill road to Naini Tal. It was a beautiful place, with the snow-capped Cheena Peak rising to 8,000 feet in the north, and nine lakes in the valley. On one of those lakes was the world's highest yacht club and in the town were a polo ground, a Christian church and a Buddhist temple – where the bells rang twenty-four hours a day. We could see all that as we climbed the final 1,600 feet to Sherwood College on horseback, or in a rickshaw, or in a dandi – a kind of sedan chair carried by four of the coolies. The rest carried our luggage.

'It was a Diocesan Church school, with an extensive curriculum. We had maths, science, politics – particularly British Empire politics – English, Latin and Urdu. I'd learnt colloquial Urdu at home, but found the grammar, and the poetic flow and classical beauty of the script very enjoyable. All this was to prepare us boys for any career, anywhere in the world. The working language was English, and even the food was English-style – except that we were treated to Indian food about twice a week. Discipline was harsh – the masters carried Malacca canes and would flog you on the spot, just for having your hands in your pockets, or your jacket unbuttoned. I got six of the best once for letting loose a stag beetle in assembly, and another time for bunking off after lights out with my mates for an Indian meal down in the town.'

He smiles, remembering his lady art teacher:

'I was good at art. I won the prize every year – except once, when it was given to another boy. I convinced myself that that was just for form's sake.'

All sports were compulsory, including boxing. There was an annual tournament for all weights:

'The bouts were judged by the Principal from the ringside. The good boxers murdered the plodders, but if you won you got promoted to a higher grade and then risked a far bigger thumping. A good mate of mine floored me eight times, or so I was told. He said he'd tried to finish the fight off early to spare me, but the Principal wouldn't call a halt. I lost several teeth, and got a badly broken nose.

'Most of the schools had a cadet force. We joined at fifteen, and took the oath of allegiance at sixteen. It was a full military training – parades, manoeuvres, battle and combat skills, live ammo range shooting with the .303 rifle, Lewis gun and .455 revolver – all of which I'm sure we enjoyed to the full. Our role was to provide the second line of defence to back up the regular army. We also attended parades on royal occasions and public events. We were known as the AFI – Auxiliary Force India. More than once we paraded in the rear of the army confronting political agitators – in full uniform with fixed bayonets, and four clips of five rounds in our webbing pockets.'

Colin enjoyed the cadet life, particularly the shooting – he was a crack shot from his hunting forays with his father. He also enjoyed, with his mates, parading in full uniform for Sunday church, saluting the flag on Armistice Day, and showing off to the girls of All Saints'. In church they sat in their segregated pews and were strictly off limits – but that was not the case when they got a day off at weekends and on holidays during term time, when socialising in town was quite enjoyable. And, of course, during the three month annual break, the Delhi social life at home and around town was something to look forward to.

At school, Colin continued his adventures:

'I was on the edge of the woods, collecting beetles. I stood up to ease my back, and there, not three yards away, glaring at me, was a thumping great black panther. What I should have done was to stand my ground and stare him out, but I panicked – turned and ran like hell. They reckoned I was lucky and it was yelling like a maniac that saved me.'

He survived to finish his education in 1940. Vic had already volunteered for the Army Medical Corps, and other mates had already joined up, so when he got home to Delhi, he applied to the Royal Air Force. It took until July 1941 for him to be duly declared European according to the requirements of the National Service Act (European British Subjects) 1940, and available for service. He was invited to a medical in Burmah Shell House, Delhi:

There, they found that my broken nose was a complication, so I had to have it fixed – it took to the end of the year. I didn't recover until the following March.

He was then ordered to report to the Initial Training Wing (ITW) in Lahore:

'There were no aptitude tests, and no aircraft either except for one grounded Wapiti – I sat in it every day and went through the drills. I enjoyed the theory and came out in the top six in the exams. But then they decided to post those six for immediate training as observers. We were devastated. We marched straight off to protest to the boss. Didn't do any good though. The CO tried to sell it to us that as observers we'd get a good deal of piloting anyway – but it scuppered my dreams of Spitfires and Hurricanes.'

Colin was at ITW from March to June 1942. It was here he made friends with Charlie Mann from St Paul's College, Darjeeling – they would serve together on 31 Squadron and be mates for life:

'At the end of June we were transferred to No. 1 Service Flying Training School at Umbala, for navigation, bomb aiming, photo reconnaissance, and wireless operation – I got to seventeen words a minute in Morse. There were dual control Hawker Harts for air gunnery, and for relief pilot instruction. So I did manage to get my hands on the stick after all.'

On 14 December 1942, aged just twenty, he was awarded his observer's brevet and sergeant's stripes. Two days later, his group was transferred to the Armament Training Unit at Bhopal, where he had his first encounter with Vickers Gas Operated (VGO) machine guns, practising from the back seat of a Hart, squirting shells at a towed drogue. After that it was the Ground Reconnaissance and Advanced Navigation School in Bombay for square searches, bombing, gunnery and navigation. On 20 April 1943, Colin's training was complete:

'We'd been at it for over a year, and it turned out to be the last observer intake in the RAF – the Air Ministry binned it as being too long and too expensive. Because of that, and as the course was so comprehensive, our observer's brevets became a badge of distinction. For us, that made up a lot for the disappointment of not making it as fighter pilots.'

He now grabbed a couple of weeks' leave, at home in Delhi, where the war was not very much in evidence, and sport and partying continued in full swing. But many of the Germans who had been part of the scene were not around any more – they'd been interned for the duration.

In May, Sergeant Lynch left Delhi, to join 31 Squadron and its Dakotas. Within three days of his arrival, he was sent on detachment, with 'B' Flight, to the supply dropping base at Agatarla, behind the Chin Hills and 120 miles west of the Burmese border. The monsoon season had just started.

Chapter 10

Air Dropping at Tiddim

As Colin Lynch arrived at Agartala, Peter Bray had just been appointed 'B' Flight Commander in the rank of acting squadron leader:

'The Squadron Headquarters had been moved forward to Karaghpore, west of Calcutta. When we got there we found pretty good conditions – bashas made of bamboo and palm leaf and each hut had its own Indian bearer. There were decent charpoys to sleep on and a cabinet for your things. You could even take a shower – old petrol cans of water, with holes punched in them. I didn't have to make much effort where discipline was concerned – everyone was much too busy to waste time messing around.'

He was starting an operational tour of 500 hours:

'But only "active service" hours on supply drops in Burma, troop ferrying and paratroop dropping counted to this total. Passenger, freight and mail run hours in India didn't – and there were plenty of those. Nor did the hundred or more sorties that I logged in May and June, converting new aircrews to the Dakota.

'We flew practically continuous supply dropping sorties from our detachment airfield at Agartala and from another at Tetspor. The main hazard in the air was the weather – the monsoon was well under way in May and the storms were exceptionally dangerous. They were even a danger to life on the ground. I got a shock, in more ways than one, when lightning struck the Ops Room table. It was by a fluke that the bolt went to ground and left us untouched.'

The crewing system on RAF Dakotas was first pilot – who was the aircraft captain – a second pilot, navigator, and two wireless operators. When he arrived on strength at Agatarla, Colin Lynch was crewed primarily as a navigator:

'We were billeted in bashas, which had mud banked up at the sides in an attempt to keep the floods out – and the cows too. They didn't always work and we'd often get back from a trip to find that the sacred beasts had left their calling cards on the floor.

'We flew on most days. When we had a really early take-off, I'd sleep in my clothes, ready to go. We had khaki flying suits, designed to give us some kind of jungle camouflage. We'd get an early call from one of the duty airmen with a hurricane lamp – there was no electricity in the camp – and grab an early breakfast. I'd slap on my jungle hat, and strap on my standard issue sidearm – at first it was an Enfield .38 revolver, but later we got the much more useable Smith and Wesson. In my belt I'd have a kukri knife, a dagger and a folding machete. And of course I'd make sure my ammo pouch was full. Loaded down, we were. The only thing we didn't carry at that time was personal parachutes – but we got them later. I'd squeeze myself into my seat and off we'd go, to navigate around the mountains and jungle.'

The charts were serviceable – Assam and Burma had been pretty well surveyed before the war – with one in a million scale for high level navigation and a quarter inch to the mile for map reading. Rather than taking time to circle the airfield to climb for height, the Dakotas would set course from take-off, and the navigator would calculate the winds at altitude. Magnetic variation was just one degree east and could be ignored, but magnetic deviation was something else again. When the load was a Jeep and trailer, the compass was all over the place. There was an invaluable telescopic device mounted alongside the navigator's table, pointing down below the fuselage to give a sight of the ground. Gridlines on the instrument gave a reading of drift – essential in the 'dead reckoning' of the heading to be flown.

Checking with his logbook, Peter Bray recalls sorties to Tiddim:

'If the weather was good, there wasn't much to do in the way of navigation – the maps were clear and apparently accurate, and after a couple of trips we could recognise the route. My Canadian warrant officer second pilot was a dab hand at tracking the mountain ranges and rivers. The Dakota had no trouble climbing to the 7,500 feet we needed to clear the Chin Hills and after an hour or so we could see the Manipur River ahead, running across our track. We just had to turn to starboard and follow it southwards to find Tiddim, at 4,000 feet, on top of a pine covered mountain. There was a zigzag dirt road up the side – climbing 2,000 feet in four miles. The DZ was a bit further on, a quarter mile long natural clearing on a ridge overlooking the river. We set up a circuit at five to six hundred feet, while three of the crew – usually the nav and the two W/Ops – got the load ready in the back.'

'Para-packs', with tinned and packaged rations, clothing, ammunition or fuel, were pushed out of the freight door as the Dak flew straight and level over the DZ at around 300 feet. On some runs, soft goods – rice, flour or soya – were 'free-dropped' from a much lower level, 50 feet or so. They were in triple bags made of jute. The idea was that on impact the outer would be destroyed, the next might be damaged but the inner should remain intact.

The dispatchers would manhandle the first of the packs, chute on top, and weighing in at well over 100lbs, to the sill of the door – always open, ready to go. The static line would be hitched to a roof cable, and a dispatcher would stand on each side of the pack, while another sat behind, feet up against it and back against the fuselage wall. There they would wait – eyes on the two lights above the door.

The Dakota would be brought onto the approach into wind, and at about 100 yards from the dropping point it was 'red light on', and the dispatchers would brace themselves ready. At the green light, it was time to heave, the man at the back shoving with every ounce of strength his legs could muster, and out the pack would shoot into the slipstream. The static line yanked the chute open, and down the pack floated.

The lead dispatcher would lean out of the door and check on the drop's progress. If it was in the middle he'd give the thumbs up to the pilot and round they'd go again – and again and again, for up to two dozen passes, and for anything up to an hour or more. Then, it was back to base – through the weather and the Japanese fighters.

Colin Lynch was to carry out many air drops at Tiddim:

'At our cruising speed of 150 knots, and say thirty minutes for dropping, we averaged two and a half hours per round trip, sometimes twice and even three times in a day. Seven days a week there was the same routine. After take-offs at 06.30 and 10.30, there was a short lunch break, then a final take-off at 14.30. In my logbook are eighty-seven sorties to Tiddim from June to September 1943, and in all there were 109.'

That allowed plenty of opportunity for trouble, and sure enough, trouble there was:

'Halfway through a drop at Tiddim, one chute opened just outside the doorway. Its static line was too short. The whole lot smashed into the tailplane. Outside I could see rigging lines streaming around the elevator, with the chute on the top and the pack underneath. The impact had bent up the tailplane leading edge and the parachute was blanking off the elevator. That gave the pilot, Vern Rutherford, a problem in controlling height, so we had to shift the packs we had left backwards and forwards to get the balance right. But with the dodgy elevator, Vern couldn't get the aircraft to climb. It was pretty hairy – we had to get back over those mountains to make it home to base. Well, with the second dickie sitting there calling on all the gods he could think of, Vern got us over those ridges. We just scraped it – literally, because at

Agartala we burst through the last line of trees before the runway. Putting the flaps down would have upset the trim, so it was a very high-speed landing, finishing with a ground loop to stop. Old Vern was in shock – had to be helped off the aircraft.'

Alongside the air drop sorties, Colin and crew did their share of the regular mail runs:

'We'd fly first thing in the morning to Calcutta to collect mail, passengers and freight, and then on to all the half dozen forward bases. At each one we'd land, unload and load, before taking off to the next. Then it was back to Calcutta before finally returning to base at Agartala. It took all day.'

The mail runs, like all flying in this theatre, were not without hazard. One sortie was to take a Jeep and a cargo of high-ranking officers back to Calcutta, and should have been straightforward. But it was from a short jungle strip. The pilot didn't quite make it over the trees and took the tip off the starboard wing. They got back in one piece, with just a bit of help from the aircrew, and a lot from the good old Dakota.

'It was a terrifically robust aeroplane. We were often hit by gunfire and landed with bullet holes in the airframe – once we got a hole as big as your fist from a mortar shell. Then the Japs used to stretch half inch cables across the valleys to deter fighter-bombers. On one sortie we hit one. The pro-pellers cut off a length of the cable which lodged on the pitot head and the Dak landed with cable streaming back from the nose, beating a tattoo on the airframe. The props had suffered just a couple of dents – nothing to stop us being ready for the next sortie.

'Those props and the engines were tough. Once, on a long-range penetration sortie in the Arakan, we had a vulture strike. The unfortunate bird penetrated past the propeller – losing its head on the way – and lodged in the nacelle. But the engine kept going, and the remains of the bird were dug out after landing.'

It took a lot to bring the Dak down, but Colin and his colleagues knew that from time to time the weather, or enemy action, could be fatal:

'Generally we aircrews were kept in the dark about who we were dropping to, in case of a forced landing and being captured and interrogated by the Japs. We'd all heard about their horrific treatment of prisoners, alive or dead. They seemed to think that killing just wasn't enough. How did such a cultured and artistic nation get to be so brutal?

'We thought about that on the long-range sorties we did that summer of '43, down on the Arakan Front, where the Allies were holding the line. They were codenamed 'Epigram', those trips, and they took three hours plus. We often had fighter escorts by day – RAF Hurricanes and then later in the year, Spitfires, and American Thunderbolts and Mohawks. But we never had fighter cover at night.'

Colin submitted a flightlog to Operations after every sortie. After the last one of the day, or on the odd occasion when he wasn't flying, there might be time for some relaxation:

'I spent quite a few of my hours off with my feet up on my charpoy in the basha. I used to play my harmonica a lot. Sometimes we'd take a longish walk to the local village, Singabil. It was really no more than a single street of bamboo huts on stilts, but it had a blacksmith – he made me a cus-tomised kukri complete with scabbard. There was also a boatyard where you could hire a small kishti for a fishing trip, and a Chinese café where you could have a duck egg omelette for breakfast. As for entertainment, we didn't often stay late in Singabil – the street took on a dodgy atmosphere after dark. You know what I mean? If we wanted, and had a bit of leave, we could go on the mail run aircraft to and from Calcutta for the shopping – and social activities.'

Throughout 1943, 31 Squadron was largely on its own in the business of supply dropping in Burma. The heavy workload of sorties continued throughout the year in the most hazardous flying conditions imaginable – monsoon weather and thundercloud turbulence, mountains up to 8,000 feet, and enemy fighters and ground fire. Colin was aware of the risks:

'Until our fighter pilots drove the Japanese raiders back to their rear bases our Dakotas were sitting ducks for air attack. On operational flights there were always two VGOs stowed by the open port and starboard main body windows. To use them, you'd lift them onto a swivel mount, so that the barrel pointed out behind the wing. They carried a 100 round spring magazine, tensioned by a handle on top – there were several mags for each gun. There was a heavy duty deflector bag attached to the ejection port, to collect spent cartridges. They were intended for defensive purposes only, and we had been trained for air to ground and air to air deflection firing. The W/Ops and I did a good deal of air gunnery practice on the squadron – just in case.

'At the end of November, I was transferred to Flying Officer Larsen's crew, and a week later we were on an early morning mission headed for Tiddim yet again, carrying para packs, each with 1,000 rounds of .303 ammunition, crated in wood and heavy – so they had two chutes. I remember that at this stage we felt that we were just flying to the office each day – any strain was from the monotony of the routine. But 28 November was a fateful day.

'We got to Tiddim without trouble, reduced height, checked the ground signal by the DZ, and went into the circuit at 300 feet. Another Dakota was there already, with Flight Sergeant Richards – from my basha – flying it.

'Larsen was lining up behind Richards to approach the DZ, when there was a rattle of anti-aircraft fire from the ground. At the same time, through the windscreen, we could see three Jap dive bombers, escorted by four Oscar fighters, attacking the DZ. Before we could blink, three of the fighters peeled away, and opened fire on our Daks from behind.

'Bursts shot past on both sides, but not one hit us! But Richards was hit – his aircraft burst into flames and veered out of control across the valley. We banked hard right and swooped down low over the river to try to lose the fighters. As we did so, we saw the other Dak hit the cliff across the far bank and blow up.

'We flew as low over the river as we dared to evade the fighters, loading the two VGOs with a pan of ammo each. When test firing, one of the guns jammed. I spent a few minutes clearing the jam before firing another burst – and the Dakota started to corkscrew all over the place. I dashed up into the cockpit and found that the pilot had taken my second test burst for another fighter attack and so was taking evasive action. Somehow, we escaped without a scratch.

'It was very quiet in the basha that night. Flight Sergeant Richards's cheerful Scottish voice was no more.'

With the USAAF committed to the Hump operation, it had been left largely to the Dakotas of 31 Squadron – assisted by those few Hudsons of 194 during the First Chindit venture – to mount the air supply operations that kept the Allied troops in the field, guarding the northern borders of Burma. But by the end of 1943, three more RAF squadrons had joined the tactical transport force. Two of them, 194 and 62, converted from the Hudson to the Dakota and began paratroop and supply drop training at the Parachute Training School at Chaklala, in North-West India. Earlier in the war, it was 62 Squadron that from Singapore, had mounted brave attacks on Japanese shipping, before losing most of its aircraft to the Zeros. The aircrews of 117 Squadron had flown freight and passenger services in the Western Desert, with DC-2s, before moving to India, with Dakotas, at the end of the year. At the turn of 1944, all four squadrons stood ready on the northern borders of Burma, to support a planned counterattack by the newly-created Fourteenth Army, on the Japanese invaders, in the spring.

Air-drop south of Irrawaddy. (*RAF Air Historical Branch*)

Mobile Bath Unit arrives at forward airstrip. (*IWM CF222*)

Struggling in pre-monsoon winds. (*IWM CF521*)

267 Squadron joins the action. (*Derrick Hull*)

Derrick Hull at work.
(*Derrick Hull*)

Hull brothers at Mingaladon RAF base,
Rangoon. (*Richard Hull*)

Repatriation by 'Dakota Airways'. (*RAF Air Historical Branch*)

Norman Currell (centre) 'Invades Sarawak'. (*Norman Currell*)

Eric Knowles and Dakota at Battle of Britain Memorial Flight. (*Jenny Annett*)

John Hart carries British Legion banner. (*John Hart*)

Peter Bray, retired.
(*Peter Bray*)

Burma Stars at Firle Place, Sussex. Ken Brown, Henry Stock and George Hufflett meet Dame Vera. (*Kate Eastman*)

Chapter 11

The Second Battle of the Arakan

In circulation among the troops and airmen in Burma as the battles raged, were broadsheet daily newspapers, selling for one anna, about one British old penny. Paper bound pamphlets sold for eight, and all of them aimed to give the soldiers, sailors and airmen in the field good news – when good news started to arrive – to boost their morale. Those stored away in the files at the RAF Historical Branch smelled musty, as if from jungle mould, and reeked of the atmosphere of an army, navy and air force far from home. Perhaps they had been part of a load air dropped in the field? Well furnished with maps and pictures, they were published under the name of South-East Asia Command – SEAC.

SEAC was an Anglo-American creation initiated at the Allies' Quebec Conference in August 1943, establishing a joint command for all the Allied forces – land, sea and air – in the theatre. The man appointed to run it was the forty-three year old Admiral Lord Louis Mountbatten. His orders from the Chiefs-of-Staff at Quebec were 'to defend India's borders and to maintain and broaden contacts with China'. Mountbatten expanded this to require 'the re-conquest of enough of north-east Burma to safeguard the air-route over the Hump and subsequently to reopen the Burma Road'. At this stage, for the highest political reasons, there was no mention of the re-conquest of the whole of Burma.

SEAC went about its tasks with a will. British and American staffs were integrated and Lieutenant General 'Speck' Wheeler was appointed Principal Administrative Officer. He, whose 'word in priorities is to be law', had the daunting task of increasing many times over the flow of supplies to the armies in the field. This required the 800 miles of the narrow gauge Bengal and Assam Railway to be 'militarised', and 4,000 men in half a dozen US Railway Battalions were tasked with doubling the line's capacity from its 90,000 tons a month. Militarised roads to the front were also needed, and immediately the tea planters of Assam responded to the call, raising labour detachments totalling 70,000 men. They set about building a 150 mile highway from the railhead, Dimapur, down the length of Manipur state to Tamu. By the autumn, they had progressed so well that half the men could be spared for the levelling of nine Hump airfields and four fighter strips in Assam, under American direction.

In the First Arakan offensive, for every Allied battle casualty there had been 120 more incapacitated by sickness. SEAC created a Medical Advisory Division to look for ways to control malaria, dysentery, scrub typhus and other virulent jungle diseases, by spraying with DDT, by daily dosing with mepacrine (a UK manufactured substitute for quinine) and by strict prophylactic disciplines. With these precautions in place, Mountbatten planned for Allied troops to fight in malarial and disease ridden areas. By compelling the Japanese, who had few medical resources, to fight in these 'death-valleys', he intended to 'enlist malaria as an ally'.

Appointed Deputy Supreme Allied Commander to Mountbatten was Lieutenant General Stilwell, who was building up his Northern Combat Area Command (NCAC) – American and Chinese forces – preparing to push a road down the valleys out of Ledo in north-east Assam into Burma. They aimed to join up, some 300 miles south, with the Burma Road.

The Commander-in-Chief of British Land Forces was General Sir George Giffard. It was he who had to secure the resources that the newly created Fourteenth Army needed for its job – to counterattack in Burma. To command this army, headquartered in Manipur and dispersed through the Chin Hills, Mountbatten chose General Bill Slim.

The Supreme Commander had already served thirty years in the Royal Navy, and for two years had been Chief of Combined

Operations – commando actions launched by sea and air. This led most people, including the enemy to suppose that the Allies were planning a seaborne assault on Burma and, in fact, landing ships and craft were already on their way out east. But Mountbatten was also convinced of the vital part that the air had to play in jungle warfare and pressed for more aircraft, including transports. In December, the Allied air forces in SEAC were integrated, with Air Chief Marshal Sir Richard Peirse appointed as Air Commander-in-Chief.

The SEAC Commanders were impressed by the Hump operation's success in maintaining a remote army in the field, and re-doubled their efforts to build a capability in air supply. No less than 5 per cent of India's output of cloth was commandeered for parachutes and 400 powered sewing machines were sent out from England to make them. Those chutes – Irvin 'R' type – were often in short supply, so the Fourteenth Army experimented with Slim's opportunist attempt to complement them with chutes made from jute. These 'parajutes' were not a long-term success – they were like sponges when it rained – but they filled a short-term gap. All the while, General Wheeler was stocking up the supplies that would be needed for air drops in the planned offensive in 1944.

Working hard to bolster the fighting spirit of the men and their officers, Mountbatten had begun visiting regiments and squadrons within days of arriving in India and now set out to tell the troops and airmen what was planned for the coming campaign. In his distinctive white naval uniform, he would stop at the roadside to chat to a small group of soldiers, or visit a base to address a few hundred together. Standing high on an ammunition box, his words were inspiring:

'Who started this story about the Jap Superman? I have seen the Japs in Japan. Millions of them are unintelligent slum-dwellers, with no factory laws, no trades unions, no freedom of speech, nothing except an ignorant fanatical idea that their Emperor is God. Intelligent free men can whip them every time.

'We have got anti-malarial devices and we shall have the finest hospitalisation and air evacuation scheme that the Far East has ever seen. The Japs, who have nothing, will have to fight Nature as well as us.

'If they try their old dodge of infiltrating behind you and cutting your line of communication, stay put – we will supply you by air, there will be no retreat.

'We are not going to quit fighting when the monsoon comes, like drawing stumps at a cricket match when it rains. If we only fight for six months in the year the war will take twice as long. The Japs don't expect us to fight on – they will be surprised and caught on the wrong foot.'

On 10 January 1944, these words were printed in the first SEAC newspaper that floated down by parachute to the forward Fourteenth Army positions. The same edition reported an Allied advance in the Arakan.

It was in this Second Arakan Offensive that George Hufflett got his first sight of the Japanese:

'There was no frontline as such, the Japs could turn up anywhere. It was pretty clear what we had to do – take and defend those tunnels. But we'd no real idea what else was going on.'

He found himself in the middle of the first stage of the Allied grand plan to liberate Burma. Intelligence reports suggested that the Japanese army commanders were consolidating their position on the far side of the Chindwin, planning in the spring, with their reinforcements, aircraft and supplies in place, to sweep on into India. They believed that no army could counter-attack and recapture Burma, a country of mountains and jungle, from the north. Mountbatten and his staff reckoned to take them by surprise.

He had staked a lot on an amphibious attack down the coast but at the Teheran Conference at the end of November all available landing craft had been allocated to European waters. In north Burma, Stilwell had begun his long march from Ledo over the mountains. So, to disrupt the enemy's plans, Slim ordered the 5th and 7th Indian Divisions to push down the Mayu Peninsula. Their aims were to secure the mouth of the Naf River so that supplies could come in by sea, and to break the enemy's hold on the Maungdaw-Buthidaung road, a vital sixteen mile metalled highway that ran laterally across their front. It was the tunnels on this road that were the target for George's 1st Queen's, in the 7th Indian Division.

The Mayu Peninsula is split north to south along most of its 100-mile length by the 7,000-feet Mayu Range, and the tunnels were the only convenient route for moving troops across the knife edged mountains. But the Japanese held the heights over-looking the road and had turned the tunnels into a fortress. The first step was to liberate Maungdaw, a rice port on the Naf River to the west, and Buthidaung on the east of the range, which had already been fought over and was said to be the most bombed village in Burma. So while the 81st West African Division (George's black shipmates) were sent down the Kaladan Valley to secure the left flank, it was the task of the 5th Indian Division to take Maungdaw, and of the 7th to occupy Buthidaung. George tells the story:

'We started to go forward just before Christmas. It was a bit like a grim sort of Scouting expedition, with just a pack and a shovel and no tent. No cookhouse either, and the wide game for real – with the Japs looking to slit your throat if they could. We had khaki drill long trousers and long-sleeved shirts, to keep the mozzies off – and sort of rubberized canvas jungle boots. They couldn't find a jungle hat to fit me, so it had to be a tin one. We carried a kukri, and of course our .303 rifle with a full magazine and a bandolier – and bayonet. That was it. At least the rain had stopped and we were able to dig in at night. We were on iron rations but on Christmas Day they managed to get us a bottle of Aussie beer.

'It was pretty rough going along those mountain ridges – bloomin' steep they were. And there were plenty of bamboo thickets to get through, and jungle scrub. Full of thorns, that was – tore your trousers to pieces. I was quite handy with the needle and did a lot of mending. There was this bloke called Joe Fleischer – he used to cut my hair and I'd darn his socks.

'The corporals and sergeants were all conscripts, like us – we didn't see much of the officers. There was some air action but not that much – at that stage. Once, we watched a Spitfire shooting up a Jap fighter. He got the blighter – made a big dent just along the hill.

'Then the action got pretty hot. We were pinned down by a Jap machine-gun post – dug in no more than twenty yards in front of us. It was too close for our guns to bombard it so muggins' platoon was ordered to attack it. Somehow by then I'd got hold of a Bren gun. The corporal led the way, down a dogleg sort of track in the scrub, so we had a bit of cover – but there were bullets flying all around.

'We kept low, and got right up close to the dugout without being seen. It was a big old affair, all fortified with heavy timbers and a deep trench dug in front. The corporal took a pot shot through the gun slit and I could hear a Jap yelling – so he must have got one of 'em. Then he handed me a grenade and waved me into the trench to heave it in among the buggers. I jumped down the bank – felt a bit exposed but the timbers got in their way and they couldn't get to aim downwards at me. I reckon that's what saved my skin. I lobbed the grenade in. A big explosion – and that was that. It was all over in a couple of minutes.'

George and his corporal had taken out a machine-gun nest of Japanese:

'Our ammo and rations came by mule train, down from the north. There were scores of them and they came splashing across the paddy fields at night, through the fog – so we called them the "Ghost Train". What we got to eat was mainly spam and hardtack biscuits, with the occasional tin of condensed milk. Our corporal, who was a Brummie, was a dab hand at scrounging extra stuff.

'One night, right at the beginning of February – about two in the morning – we hear what we think is the Ghost Train, but it isn't – it's the Japs. There's a whole lot of screaming and shouting – then the shooting starts. As the dawn comes up we see thousands of the little yellow devils swarming across the paddy fields – from behind our lines. I was shit-scared, I can tell you.'

What neither George nor any of his commanders knew was that the time had come for the Japanese to launch their invasion of India, along the coastal strip and mountain ranges of the Arakan. Their intention was to split the 5th and 7th Indian divisions, destroy them separately, and then drive on to Chittagong where they would cut the railway and instigate a general uprising against the British across Bengal. From there they planned to overrun the Hump airfields of Assam. They also expected to draw Slim's reserves down into the Arakan battle before launching their main blow further north, against Imphal and the heart of Manipur, to smash the centre of the Allied front. The consequences if they had succeeded would have been disastrous for the Allies. The propaganda machine in Tokyo trumpeted: 'The march on Delhi has begun.'

The enemy had planned the invasion for March 1944, but the Allied Arakan offensive had forced his hand. Throughout the previous year, the Japanese had built up their combat strength from four to eleven divisions including 100,000 crack Imperial Troops. They planned to sweep on to Chittagong by 10 February and crucially had issued just seven days' rations to their men, relying on capturing Allied supply dumps, motor transport, artillery and armour. So confident were they of success – the Allies had always crumbled before – that they threw almost all their strength into a headlong attack, leaving only one battalion in reserve.

But the 5th and 7th Indian Divisions did not crumble. With Mountbatten's words still ringing in their ears, George and his comrades-in-arms stood their ground:

'The Japs had gone quietly up the other side of the river and come down at us from behind. They'd picked up a whole bunch of refugees in the valley and the bastards had driven them down in front of them, as a screen. That was the screaming and shouting.

'We saw our officers then, all right. They got us all into a defensive position and we did some pretty frantic work on the shovels to set up at least a bit of defence. They were at us with their mortars, and their planes came roaring in with cannon and bombs.'

The 7th Indian division was under siege for two weeks or more. The main semi-fortified position was the 'Admin Box' HQ at Sinzweya, a flat area of open ground, about 1,000 yards square. Here, the Japanese had 8,000 men mounting an assault on about the same number of Allied administrative troops: signallers, pioneers, Sappers, ordnance, maintenance and medical units, mule companies and native road builders. Fortunately the total also included two battalions of infantry, the Royal West Yorks and the Gurkhas, a dozen batteries of varied artillery and two squadrons of tanks, the 25th Dragoons. The stories of the struggles of this motley group to hold off the enemy – when cooks and clerks took up rifles with the best of them – and of the appalling Japanese atrocities in the field hospitals, are among the most heroic and harrowing of the campaign.

George and his mates were dug in on a mound along the valley from the Admin Box:

'It was fairly open country – jungle scrub and paddy fields. It was all pretty basic. You could make a fire for tea if you could find any water – there wasn't much. But we did find a small stream where you could get a bit of a wash-down – no ablutions tents, or anything like that. No latrines either – after one accident I had to chuck my underpants away. Of course we had no clean clothes and we got pretty ragged. And we all had prickly heat.

'The Japs came at us all the time, day and night. They'd drive their prisoners in front of them – dreadful that was. They'd come slithering through the tiger grass, wearing hideous facemasks and whining like animals. For every one we killed there'd be two more come up. But we kept the buggers out.

'We only managed that because the RAF and the Yanks came with their transport planes and dropped ammo to us

on parachutes. Barrels of rum, and grub too – same old bully
and beans, but it was more than the Japs had.'

When the Japanese attack came in, the 7th Indian Division had
only two days' rations. But at the new Assam airstrips, Major
General Snelling, the 'Fourteenth Army's Grocer', had stock-
piled ten days' rations for 40,000 men, so before those two days
were up, the Dakotas of the combined Troop Carrier Command
were over the defensive 'Boxes' with the first air drops:

'The first lot of Dakotas got set upon by Jap fighters and shot
at from the ground – they had to scarper, without dropping.
But they were soon back – and they got through this time.
And down came the chutes all right.'

This second wave was led by General Old himself, his plane
drilled with shell splinters. Sixty tons a day were delivered to
the beleaguered defenders. 'We saw less and less of the Jap
fighters – they'd been seen off by our Hurricanes and Spitfires,
good and proper.'

The Spitfires were new additions to the Allies' air arm, and
they proved a godsend. They had the speed, rate of climb and
firepower to deal with the Oscars, provided they got the jump
on them from altitude, which they managed more often than
not. In one day, of the forty-odd Oscars that ventured over the
Arakan, around half of them were shot down, and half
damaged. The RAF lost one Spitfire. The Dakotas flew between
the anti-aircraft fire and the dogfights to deliver the goods. After
just seven days the aerial battles were over, and the Japanese
fighters had withdrawn. Without this hard-won air superiority,
the ground troops' air supply lifeline could not have been
sustained.

In a speedy outflanking move, the Japanese had cut the
Okeydoke Pass. It was still possible to supply the 5th Indian
Division, on the west of the Tamu Range, by sea, but to the east,
the 7th Indian, and the 81st West Africans over in the Kaladin
Valley, were entirely supported by the Dakotas. In this second
Arakan battle, Troop Carrier Command flew 9,000 sorties and
delivered 60 tons daily. In the whole of this effort, although

many were damaged, just one Dakota was shot down. In that
crew was Flying Officer Tom Baptie, Peter Bray's former
navigator and best man. Peter remembers his friend:

'That very day, 9 February, we'd moved 31 Squadron headquarters further forward, to join the supply-dropping
detachment at Agatarla. It had 1,000 yards of concrete
runway and was closer to the Arakan action. Tom's captain
on that fatal flight was Flight Lieutenant Walker – he pressed
on through a hail of ground fire to make the drop and was
awarded a posthumous DFC for it. Both he and Tom died of
their wounds. The very next day we abandoned daytime
drops over the Boxes because of the intensity of ground fire,
but we carried on at night just the same.

'I made my first drop there with the CO, Wing
Commander Burbury. It was quite a trick. You had to fly at
minimum height and speed, and usually make eight circuits
to get the stuff out – that gave the Nips more than half an
hour to get our range. It was always a struggle to keep the
ship in trim, what with the turbulence and the shifting load
being hauled about in the back. If you got too far out of
balance, the chute could get tangled in the rudder. At night
you had to drop on light signals and the enemy would lay
out false ones to lure you off course – that was dangerous
with the mountains so close. The lads down the back
sweated and strained to lug the 6,000lbs of packs down the
freight cabin and heave them out – being shot at all the time.
I had nothing but admiration for them.'

In the Arakan, the battle began to turn when Fourteenth Army
reinforcements were able to force their way over the mountains
from west to east. As they went, the Sappers and miners rebuilt
the dirt track into a road capable of taking tanks. That track was
the Ngakyedauk Pass – no surprise then, that George and his
mates called it the 'Okeydoke'.

Chapter 12

A Flight over the Hump

On 6 February 1944, Squadron Leader Peter Bray and his crew were withdrawn from the all out effort in the Arakan to make a sortie over the infamous Hump:

'The mission had been organised to take a British General, Carton de Wyatt, to Chungking, where he was to take up the post of British Representative at the government of Chiang Kai-shek, the Chinese leader. All very hush-hush it was, and security was tight. We'd flown the day before right up the Brahmaputra valley, to Dinjan, an RAF base being used by the USAAF for the Hump operation. At dawn we had to wait in a freezing cold cockpit out on the dispersal, surrounded by military police, until a procession of motors, bristling with armed guards, arrived with our passenger.

'It was 500 miles from Dinjan to our first stop, Kunming, and the estimated flight time was between three and four hours, depending on what winds we found at altitude. At Kunming, we'd land to drop off the mail for the RAF Signals Detachment before flying on to Chungking, Chiang's provisional capital, which was another 350 miles. On the first leg, the American airbase at Yunnanyi was the diversion – over the mountains, at 6,500 feet and about 100 miles west of Kunming on the old Burma Road. We had no diversions on the second leg – if we ran into trouble it was back to Kunming.

'To get to the altitude we needed, 16,000 feet, we were flying a Dak with two-stage superchargers. Of course we needed oxygen for everyone – that cut in at 10,000 feet. We had full fuel tanks – enough for there and back was the drill – and from the 90-feet elevation of Dinjan we had to reach 7,000 feet within fifteen minutes to clear the first ridge. That was in the Paktai range. Of course, Daks had done that hundreds of times before but for us first timers it was somewhat unnerving. We'd heard all the stories about American C-47s and C-46s leaving a trail of aluminium wreckage along the route and we were looking over our shoulders all the time for Jap fighters – they were still to be reckoned with and had been turning their attention to the top corner of Burma in recent weeks. Anyway, the super-chargers got us over the ridge all right and we headed for our first fix, the British garrisoned Fort Hertz, climbing on up to the altitude we needed for the next mountain range.

'That was the 14,000 feet Kumon Ridge, just over the upper reaches of the Chindwin. The weather wasn't too bad to start with, and we could see the Himalayas stretched out below – covered with snow and rugged as hell. Rather like the Alps but everything on so much grander a scale. I remember the Dak felt very, very small indeed. It was quite something to think that absolutely everything the Chinese and American forces fighting in China needed had been coming this way since July '42..

'In good weather, it was possible to fly the Hump at 10,000 feet, using the passes over the mountain ranges. But you had to know the terrain really well to do that, and we didn't. In any event, the weather was closing in – and it was bumpy. Actually, that's a complete understatement. There was a fair old wind at that height, on our tail – which helpfully was bringing forward our ETA Kunming – but it was blowing across the ridges, and set up these lenticular waves of air. It was like riding a gigantic, malicious big dipper – a sort of giant fist would grip the aeroplane and wrench it downwards 1,000 feet and then toss it back up again like a toy. The autopilot couldn't stay in and it was a real struggle to keep control.

'The General must have been very uncomfortable down the back. At least the crew and I could keep our minds on operating the aircraft – he just had to sit and take it. I decided to use the superchargers to clamber up to 18,000 feet – higher than I'd ever been in a Dak before – to try to get out of the turbulence.

'But then of course, we went into cloud. We knew from the chart that below us by now were the western and eastern upper valleys of the Irrawaddy, and after those would be the Salween. Past the Salween valley was the 15,000 feet Santsung range. We needed to keep on track – if we strayed south we would get uncomfortably close to the Jap airbase at Myitkyina, and to the north were some seriously high mountains. So the navigator was particularly busy. Once we were past Fort Hertz, although there was a scattering of low-frequency radio beacons along the route, it was mostly dead reckoning. He managed to use the bubble sextant in the astrodome to work out a fix just before we lost sight of the sun, but now we were flying blind, and trusting to his wizardry.

'Then suddenly, it was my turn to get busy. We began to ice up. Icing in an aeroplane is a rather unpleasant experience. Super-cooled rain freezes on impact and the ice changes the shape of the aerofoils. That reduces lift, and increases drag and weight – so down you go – and the peaks get closer. You open up the throttles to maintain airspeed – and reduce your range. The ailerons and elevators ice up too, and the controls become sloppy, and have less effect – it takes an effort to keep straight and level. None of that helps a pilot's peace of mind anywhere, but at three and a half miles above the Himalayas, it's something else again.

'Now, the Dakota was fitted with hydraulic rubber 'boots' on the leading edges of the wing, fin and tailplane – the idea was that glycol was pumped through the boots, distorting their shape and, if you were lucky, breaking the ice off. But they had to be handled with some care. I'd used them before – we got icing over Burma too – and I'd found that if you put them on and left them on, ice formed just ahead of the boots, and then they became useless. The trick was to let the ice build up to a certain extent, then put the boots into operation

– just long enough to get rid of the bulk of the ice – then go back to normal and let the ice build up again. If that technique didn't work, then you could only descend to a warmer level, where the ice would melt and fall off. Of course, that day, over the peaks of the world's highest mountains, that just wasn't an option.

'So we soldiered on, working the boots all the time, and praying that we'd come out of the clouds. From time to time we did, and in the gaps the boots cleaned us up enough to survive the next stint.

'Well, we made it across the mountains and started our descent towards Kunming. Before too long, we were able to pick up the signal from their Range Beam. That, I can tell you, was a great relief. The navigator had done a great job, and there it was, bleeping loud and clear. The arrangement is that the beacon sends out two signals, one a dash and the other a dot. All dots and you know you're to port of the track, all dashes and you're to starboard. When you get dots and dashes one after the other, you're spot on. Trouble was, the radio waves with these Range Beams were sometimes distorted by what they called splinters, set off by some big magnetic mountain, or an electric storm. But we'd been told the one at Kunming was generally reliable – it was a great comfort at the end of that gruelling ride, I can tell you.

'Kunming is itself pretty high up – at 6,200 feet – but for-tunately it was clear of cloud. We could see the Burma Road snaking along below us, and the four landmark lakes down to the south. We all kept a good lookout as we came in on the approach. On two days in December, the Japanese had sent in about seventy fighters and a dozen heavy bombers in an attempt to smash up the airfield, a key one in the Hump operation. They'd shot down some Daks, too. But we made it all right.

'The flight up to Chungking turned out to be a fairly demanding affair as well – more dead reckoning, and peaks above 10,000 feet. Mercifully, there was no ice but it was still pretty bumpy. When we got there, and the General took his leave of us, he was ashen-faced – I hope he recovered by the time he had to face Chiang. We ourselves weren't exactly on top form as we were motored off to Ops – we knew we had to go through it all again next day, back the way we came – and against the wind.'

Chapter 13

Five More go off to War

George Hufflett's family say that up to now he has buried the horrors of his wartime experiences at the back of his mind. He's never sought out old comrades and is always well occupied with the present. But now, in older age, he is becoming more forthcoming about the fighting in Burma. He mentions rare moments of relaxation, with shows laid on by the Entertainments National Services Association, ENSA:

> 'One of the few real stars to come out was Vera Lynn. They tell me we're distant relations by marriage – she only lives just along the Downs, in Ditchling. She'd have a story to tell.'

Would Dame Vera Lynn be willing to share her reminiscences of her time out there on the road? When was she there, exactly? George isn't sure, but the Burma Star Association knows.

Among battle histories and eyewitness accounts on the Association's website, are reports of battlefield visits and of continuing charity works where the name of Vera Lynn is prominent. She was presented with the Burma Star for her work in Assam, for three months from March 1944. That meant she had arrived there as George was flying up to reinforce the line behind Imphal and the Japanese were launching their 'March on Delhi'. She must have seen so much.

A letter to Dame Vera Lynn DBE, Ditchling, Sussex gets an immediate, and positive response. Yes, she'd be willing to contribute to a book about Burma, and yes, she'd be happy to be interviewed – next week would be fine.

Further internet research shows that Vera was born a year

before the end of the First World War in London's East Ham to Bertram and Annie Welch. She studied dancing as a child and began singing in public aged just seven. By the time she was eighteen she'd adopted her maternal grandmother's maiden name as her stage name, and was singing with the Joe Loss Orchestra. By the end of the 1930s, after stints with other bands and a string of successful recordings, she was given her own radio series. She was a natural for the wireless – you could hear every word she sang and her natural, unaffected style charmed millions. She became hostess of the BBC radio programme *Sincerely Yours* in 1940, just as the dangers of war began to intensify for servicemen at home and overseas. The programme grew in popularity and she became the 'Forces' Favourite'. And she made that ENSA tour to Burma.

Her house is bright and airy, with a terrace overlooking lawns and herbaceous borders, and splendid views of the Downs. Moles have been having a field day under the grass, and she's not best pleased:

> 'I must get my son-in-law to deal with those. My daughter lives just next door, over the trees there. Her husband was in the RAF, a navigator – they met when he landed on the lawn to collect me for a charity concert.'

The living room is full of comfortable armchairs, the shelves stacked with books:

> 'Between shows in the West End I'd get out when I could and go and visit the booksellers in the Charing Cross Road. I got to know some of them quite well – found a few bargains, too.'

In the spaces between the books are a lifetime's souvenirs. She picks up a bone handled Sheffield steel knife, much battered and missing half its blade:

> 'See where it's engraved with three lots of initials? Here's the original owner, a Tommy. Here's the Jap who looted it and this is another Tommy who got it off the dead Jap.'

On the grand piano stands a photo of Dame Vera with the Queen Mother, another of her being presented to the Queen and yet another with Lord Louis Mountbatten:

'He came to hear me sing in Burma. I met Lady Mountbatten too, at a hospital in Dimapur – and Lady Slim. Apart from the brave Queen Alexandra's nurses, they were the only women I saw out there.'

It was early in 1944 when Vera Lynn offered her services to ENSA:

'I said I didn't want to go where there were a lot of enter-tainers already. Where could I go where no one else would? They said, "Well, there's Burma." So I said, "All right then." The British Cabinet weren't so sure about me going – all those men and that sort of thing. I said, "Look, I've been singing in workingmen's clubs since I was seven – I can handle myself, don't you worry"'

There were also worries that her kind of sentimental song might make the boys more homesick and damage their morale:

'I told them my songs were heard all the time by the boys. My radio shows were beamed everywhere overseas, and they were very popular, even in occupied Europe – they listened to them precisely to keep their spirits up.'

The tour went ahead. She was first kitted out in 'Basil dress' (named after Basil Deane, the Director of ENSA) which was the blue battledress for Europe:

'But that was no good for Burma. For that I was given khaki drill trousers, skirt and shirt – and some of those shorts. You know, the ones with the very wide legs. They didn't have my size so I had to fold the waist over and tuck it up into a belt. They paid me twenty pounds a week – I passed that on to my pianist. I never took money for entertaining the troops.'

She had the necessary injections and was told not to keep a diary, for security reasons:

'I did, though – in a little red book.'

Three days after her twenty-seventh birthday, she left her husband of two years at home:

'Harry was a tenor saxophonist – he was one of the original RAF Squadronnaires, a swing-band made up from eight members of the Ambrose orchestra.'

Accompanied by her pianist, Len Edwards and his mini piano, she embarked on an RAF Sunderland flying boat:

'It took us nine hours to get to Gibraltar – we had to fly all the way out into the Atlantic and then right round Spain. I've never been in anything more uncomfortable in my life – so noisy, and just metal seats to sit on. And the weather was rough. In Basra, there was a storm and the water got so choppy we couldn't take-off. We'd had to get down to the shore at three in the morning – then we were sent back to the hotel and sat twiddling our thumbs for hours.

'At all the bases and hospitals en route we gave shows, once during a sandstorm. That one should have been a big open air do, but we had to cram into a tent and give the performance three times over.'

In Bombay they transferred to a Dakota and flew to Chittagong, where they were handed over by ENSA to the care of the Army:

'The piano was manhandled into the back of a Jeep, Len strapped an army revolver onto his belt, and we were off. We entertained troops and airmen at camps, airfields and hospitals. Our mini piano took some punishment and often broke down. The keyboard got clogged with swarms of great big beetles – the arc lights attracted them. I could hear their creepy feet and wings scratching the keys, and then they'd get caught in my hair. I soon took to wearing a jungle cap.'

Vera found the heat and humidity stifling – a real challenge for a singer:

'I was only allowed to take one small canvas bag, so I'd put in just the one dress, my pink chiffon – cost me a whole year's clothing coupons. I tried to wear it from time to time, for a bit of glamour, but I had to spray it with water to keep me cool, and it got rather too clingy for comfort – and decency. So I stuck mostly to the khaki shirt and trousers, and now and again, those shorts.'

At dusk and in the early mornings, when the mosquitoes were at their most troublesome, she regularly heard, 'Roll your sleeves down, Vera!'

'Our shows were usually about an hour long, sometimes for thousands in the open air and sometimes in a hospital for a dozen or so. Once I sang for just two badly wounded boys on stretchers. Sadly, one of them didn't pull through. We gave a performance for the West Africans – they called me their "White Mumma" – and another for a bunch of sparky infantry lads. They managed to find a double meaning in the words of *If I had my way* – we had a good laugh at that.'

There was constant dosing with salt tablets, and the food was memorable for its dullness:

'Soya links – a kind of sausages – were the usual, and then plain boiled rice with a dollop of jam. There was some soup, which came smothered with flies – you had to push those away with your spoon. But the army did its best to make us as comfortable as possible and usually I had a tent of my own, even decorated with a little jar of jungle flowers – but once I had to make do with a hospital stretcher set up across two chairs. That was where they presented me with a Jap bullet they'd just taken out of a wounded soldier – took me back a bit, that did.

'I had a bucket of water for washing in, and just had to deal with my laundry when I could. I did manage a swim in the sea at Cox's Bazaar, and that was lovely! We had Gurkhas to guard us at the concerts – just as well because in the Arakan we got down to within six miles of the tunnels and the front line.'

Mention of the Arakan prompts thoughts of George, and triggers an idea. Maybe Dame Vera would like to meet some of the Burma veterans who lived in her local area? Perhaps we could set up a small reunion? 'I'll go anywhere for the boys,' she says.

The prospect of such a gathering finds favour with the editor of *Sussex Life* magazine, and he is glad to commission an article, plus photographs, on 'Burma Stars in Sussex', for the September edition. All being well, George and a few others will have at least a full colour feature on their time spent fighting in the 'Forgotten War' to show their grandchildren.

Ken Brown, now President of the Brighton and Hove Branch of the Burma Star Association, holds details of all the members living in Sussex, and after several phone calls and a good deal of networking, in the July heat wave of 2006 (good Burma weather), three old soldiers – Henry Stock from Shoreham, Ken Brown from Brighton and George Hufflett – team up with Dame Vera for a photo shoot.

Viscount Gage kindly hosts a tea party on the terrace of his ancestral home, Firle Place and, while the *Sussex Life* photographer busies herself with making the most of the brilliant light and the array of medals, the veterans talk modestly of their time in Burma. It turns out that all three had been in the battles on the Burma-Assam border in 1944, and within earshot of Dame Vera. More experiences and memories are shared later at the Ram Inn, where George and Henry discover they had both joined up in the Royal Sussex, and Ken Brown tells them he had been in the Royal Signals:

'I wanted to be a dispatch rider but they were looking for potential paratroopers. My glasses saved me from that, so after I'd scored 100 per cent on a simulated Morse test I was sent off for eight weeks' basic and then five months' signals training. We were at a commandeered holiday camp in Prestatyn – lived like kings we did, three to a chalet. After a spell at a posting division in Norfolk we got fourteen days' embarkation leave. That meant only one thing in those days – service abroad, and we sailed for India in July '43.

'A month before me,' says George. 'Did you sail from the Clyde, too?'

'No, we went from Liverpool, on a 22,000-ton troopship, the *Maloja*. Packed it was, with 5,000 Army, 1,000 RAF, and 800 in the ship's company. We went out into the Atlantic, and then right down to Freetown Bay on the African coast. It took us nine weeks to reach Bombay, but our first landfall was Durban.'

'I was there,' says George.

'So was I,' adds Henry. 'I went on the old *Athlone Castle* – no pleasure trip, that.'

'The people in Durban were more than friendly,' continues Ken. 'They were there waiting in their cars at the docks, offering hospitality at their homes. And then, do you remember "The Lady in White?"' They do remember, and tell Dame Vera all about her.

During, and after the war, hundreds of ships passed through Durban harbour, their decks packed with soldiers, sailors and airmen – and casualties – all in various states of emotional turmoil. From April 1940, each vessel was welcomed by South Africa's own Vera Lynn. A soprano, Perla Sielde Gibson, dressed all in white, would sing patriotic songs from the quayside, her powerful voice rising above the clamour of the dockyards. She was a fifty year old mother of three, who had lost one of her sons in the war, a fact that without doubt added to the poignancy of her performances.

'She sang us in and she sang us out,' says Ken. 'Her voice carried over the water until we were long past the harbour bar – wasn't a dry eye on board.'

All of them, including Dame Vera, had their first sight of the sub-continent in Bombay, the 'Gateway to India'. Ken remembers it without affection:

'It was persisting down with rain, and an old native spat at us from the quay. So this is India, I thought.'

Dame Vera tells them about her airsickness during the flying boat trip, George his brush with malaria, and Henry, his attack of prickly heat in the Secunderabad garrison.

'I went first to the garrison in Poona,' says Ken. 'We had a terrific Christmas dinner, served by the officers. But it didn't do a lot for our appetites when one of the stewards said, "Don't make a mess of the white tablecloths – they've got to go back to the mortuary in the morning."'

George speaks a bit about his adventures in the Arakan, and the tunnels.

'I was at those tunnels!' exclaims Henry. 'We'd been sent down in 36th Div from the reserve at Chittagong to flush the Japs out. A hell of a fight it was. It took days to blast them out of their bloomin' great dugouts – but we got 'em in the end.'

'By then I'd been flown up to Kohima,' adds George. That's when he and Ken find out they'd been within a few foxholes of each other in that epic struggle.

'I went to all those places,' chips in Dame Vera.

When it is time for her to say goodbye and her car drives away, it's with more than a little affection that the three old soldiers hum a few bars of *We'll Meet Again*.

Finishing their drinks, George, Ken and Henry wonder how many others like them are scattered across the country – men who made it home and are still alive to tell the tale.

One such is Eric Knowles. In his 82nd year, he works at least one day a week a long way from Sussex in the Visitor Centre at the Battle of Britain Memorial Flight.

One Tuesday morning, during a tour of the hangar and a clamber aboard the Dakota, he shares some of his vivid memories of trooping flights in that iconic aircraft – in Burma. Soon, over a cup of coffee, he is recounting his experiences as a young soldier in 1944 and '45, in the 3rd of Foot, Royal East Kents, 'The Buffs', and telling the story of how he got there:

'We come from the East End – my paternal great-grandfather was the last in a long line of Knowles who were fishermen in Barking. The "Barking Smacks" were the pride of Billingsgate fish market in the nineteenth century. They had a seawater tank in the hold which meant they could deliver the herring fresh, first thing in the morning – they coined it until steam came along.'

Eric's great-great-grandfather had gone to work one day in 1810 and came back seven years later – he'd been press ganged onto one of His Majesty's frigates:

'That was the first military Knowles that I know of. In the First World War my dad was in the Machine Gun Corps in the 16th Irish Division, in the thick of the action, from Passchendaele to the first breaking of the German lines in August 1918, and then on to victory – but very near the end he got gassed. After the war, he found a job driving a bakery's delivery van.

'I won a scholarship to Wanstead County High School and, when there were mass evacuations after the retreat from Dunkirk, my parents decided I should stay put. But the school had to close and it wasn't until January 1940 that I picked up my education again. I went with the stragglers from half a dozen other schools, all lumped together into a reopened Wanstead High.'

That was the first disruption to Eric's schooling – the next was the Blitz:

'After all the chaos and narrow escapes, I'd had enough of school. I went to work in the newspaper industry, but when the bombing in London picked up again in '43, I went for a Boy Entrant in the Army. I needed my father's signature to apply, and that wasn't so easy to get – he told me that he hadn't fought the war to end all wars only to let his son get caught up in another politicians' war so soon. But we could both see there was a chance that when I was called up at eighteen I could draw the short straw and become a Bevin Boy, down the pits. Anything was better than that, so he signed.'

Eric passed the medical and in November reported first to the barracks in Canterbury, and then to the Boys' Battalion training camp at Herne Bay:

'After being chased about a bit in the normal military manner, we progressed through standard infantry, corps, and battalion training, and passed out as riflemen in March 1944. We were several weeks at a holding battalion, before getting fourteen days' embarkation leave, after which I left – with hugs from my mum and a "Keep your head down" from my dad.

'We embarked at Liverpool at the end of May on the *Staffordshire* – a Bibby Line ship, painted grey for the trooping. Once on board they told us we were going to the Far East to reinforce the 2nd Battalion, which was on its way there from Iraq. I was still only seventeen and too young for active service but the sergeant said, "By the time you get there you'll be eighteen".'

The ship sailed in convoy out into the Atlantic, and then put into Freetown in Sierra Leone, but the first run ashore was in Durban, where 'Nobby', as his mates had dubbed him, was another to hear The White Lady sing:

'When we docked in Bombay we marched through a tall brick arch that they said gave the town its name – the Gateway to India. We went into the infamous Doelali Barracks for a spell, and then got sent over to the east to join up with the Buffs at Comilla, HQ of the Fourteenth Army – that was in July. Then they sent us for jungle training. "You can live on insects and roots, boys!" – that's how they gave it out. We weren't sure about that, but roughing it in swamps, elephant grass and bivouacs got us geared up all right for the action.

'They told us we were going to the Central Front – but then it all got changed. Early in '45 we were moved up to Ledo, in north-east Assam, to join the Yanks.'

Nicknames in the forces were handed out as freely as mugs of char and Arthur Watts, Ken Brown's near neighbour and

another Brighton Burma Star, was introduced as 'Benny'. He
had been in Burma as RAF ground crew:

'When I was at RAF Sealand in Shropshire, I was given the
nickname Benny by a Polish corporal who couldn't say
Arthur. He was Jewish, and I suppose he thought I was a
useful sort of bloke, so he said, "You, Benjamin, are the son
of my right hand" – and it just stuck.

'When I got to Bombay in 1943, I went by train to Number
152 Operational Training Unit. The 7th Indian Air Force was
converting to the American Vultee Vengeance dive-bomber.
We also had Tiger Moths, Dragon Rapides, Proctors, Electras
and an Anson – and I flew in all of them. Then there were the
Vickers Valencias of 31 Squadron – they were supplying the
Frontier Forts. We ground crew often had to fly on the
missions, in case of mechanical trouble. It was a long day.
We'd do Daily Inspections – DIs – at dawn, fly all the way up
there, and then, more often than not, get invited to a dining-
in night. At those, it took a strong will and stomach not to
succumb – there was a lot of spicy food, not to mention the
drink.

'When it was too hot indoors we'd take our charpoys up
onto the roof to sleep on, behind the parapets. Now, on the
floor in the bedrooms they'd painted a big white arrow,
pointing to Mecca, so you could make sure you didn't sleep
with your feet pointing that way, which would offend the
Muslims. They told us that a young newly-arrived officer
had done just that and been shot dead by a Pathan guard for
it. That was at Fort Wana, and in about 1880 – but we were
careful, all the same, up on that roof, where there wasn't a
helpful white arrow.

'At the end of the year, I put my name down for Burma. We
had to go through Calcutta, in the aftermath of a dreadful
famine. Whenever I started to feel sorry for myself after that,
I thought of those poor wretches, lying in the streets –
moaning, and starving to death.

'At Agartala, other Dakota squadrons – such as 194 – had
the Royal and the Indian Army Service Corps blokes flying
as dispatchers. Our squadron used us ground crew, and one

time, the West Africans offered to help – they were lovely guys and our CO said OK. There was a real ceremony when this big black guy joined the crew. Off he went and flew the mission – no problems. Then, when they landed, his mates were all lined up again, to meet him. He leapt off the Dakota, all smiles – and walked straight into the spinning prop. We took no more African volunteers after that.

'I was flying all the time in those planes, chucking stuff out. I helped load them, too. I can still smell the stink of vomit, fuel, sweat – and mules. They were something else again.'

Benny handed over a 3-inch square piece of blue card, with the typewritten instructions:

HOW TO LOAD A MULE
No mule is unloadable.
The recipe is as follows -
(A) Double ramp – this prevents evasion
(B) Six men pulling with ropes fastened
to the mule's elbows – not head
(C) Two men behind with a surcingle.
Using this method a mule can even
lie down. It will still go in.

Note: Do not attempt to load a
mule until several men have a grip
on the rope.
A loose mule may wreck a Dakota.

Signed: General Orde Wingate.

'To stop them braying in the jungle, they used to cut their vocal chords – poor beasts, that seemed to make them even madder. We carried a lot of them in for the Chindits.'

With mention of the Chindits, Benny's story had reached the next turning point of the Burma campaign, the launching in March 1944 of their Second Expedition behind Japanese lines. It was about this time that John Hart joined the action at RAF Imphal, as an airframe fitter. The introduction to John came from Mike Hatch, an historian at the AHB – they are both active in the British Legion in the East End, where John is one of the standard bearers on Remembrance Day parades.

A few miles east of Tower Bridge in Rotherhithe, and within a half a mile of the Thames, is where he is to be found, on a bright spring day, at home in his cottage – one of the Helen Peele Memorial Almshouses. The smart, blue-painted door is opened by an erect and well-built man. Widowed now, but fiercely self reliant in his 87th year, he offers tea and biscuits, and after some small talk about the houses and the allotment outside the window, begins to tell his story:

> 'I had two brothers and two sisters – I was the second youngest. My first school was the local primary, but at ten I went down with rheumatic fever and they moved me to a special school in the Old Kent Road – an ambulance came for me every day. I survived all that and left school at fourteen to work on the buildings – that built me up. Then at seventeen I moved indoors, working a fish and meat paste machine at Oxo, up past London Bridge. I had to leave home at six in the morning to be in time to mix the stuff up.'

At Oxo he played cricket as an all-rounder for the Works team:

> 'Lord Hawke, the Chairman of the company, was captain of England in the twenties, so playing cricket didn't do you no harm. They wanted to promote me to the Office Eleven, but I stayed with my mates in the Works team.
>
> 'My dad worked in the gasworks at Rotherhithe – a bit ironic really, as he'd been gassed in the First War. Anyhow, he died in the spring of 1939, when Hitler was getting up to all his tricks. I thought I'd better follow my dad and do my bit, so as soon as I was twenty – and we'd got my mum through the Blitz – I went for my medical.
>
> 'At a pub it was, the Yorkshire Grey in Kidbrook. I kept mum about that bout of rheumatic fever, and passed A1. My brothers were already in the army, so I put in for RAF

aircrew. They sent me off for air gunner tests in Scotland where I did all right, so next it was basic in Blackpool, then more air gunnery. My first flight, and then the training, was on the Anson and then they moved us up to the Blenheim.'

LAC Hart became a supernumerary gunner on the Lancaster, filling in the many gaps left by casualties in the regular crews of various squadrons. One of those was the renowned Number 8 Pathfinders, based at RAF Wyton in Huntingdonshire:

'While I was in the services, Oxo paid ten bob a week to my mum in lieu of my wages – more than usually generous for the times, that was. Then in 1941 I met Harriet in Birmingham and as I was dicing with bloomin' death most nights, we thought we'd better get married quick – so we did. And Oxo paid her my full wages in lieu. They were good to me, they were. The cricket might have helped.

'Any road, Jerry didn't have a flak shell with my name on it and I got through to the end of a tour. They needed reinforcements for Burma and I got posted. On Christmas Eve 1943, we marched through the streets of Liverpool in pith helmets – where they got those from beats me. We sailed on the troopship the *Queen of Bermuda* – she'd been a luxury liner before the war, so that was all right. Took us six weeks to get to India – the convoy was attacked three times by U-boats in the Bay of Biscay but we were right in the middle so they missed us. There was plenty of rough weather – the destroyers had a hard time of it in the storms, but then, so did the U-boats. I was never seasick and we had ENSA shows to help the time go by. We got through the Med, and the Suez Canal, and from Aden it was another convoy to Bombay.'

The reinforcements changed their topees for bush hats and then entrained for Assam:

'We were four ruddy days in that train – on army rations. When we stopped, we had to walk along by the tracks to reach the canteen carriage – on the way back it was a fight to keep the grub from the claws of the thieving shitehawks.

Anyway, we finally get to the railhead at Dimapur and climb into lorries for the road journey into the Chin Hills – and what a caper that was! The road had just been improved, they said – what it must have been like before, God alone knows – steep, with hairpin bends all the bloomin' way, and a sheer drop just over the side. Any road, the driver, bless him, makes it in one piece to Imphal.'

Along the road from John's almshouses, just the other side of the Surrey Docks offices is the very spot where those first bombs of the Blitz fell. It is not a great distance from there to Lambeth, the home of the Imperial War Museum. In a case are exhibits from the Burma Campaign – including Dame Vera's souvenir Jap bullet. In the two years 1942 and 1943, there were 250,000 Allied casualties from malaria, and pasted on the glass are some facts about the disease that laid George Hufflett low:

'Infection is carried by the Malarial (Anopheles) Mosquito, picked up when biting and sucking the blood of an infected victim. The native population is therefore a reservoir for the disease.

'Mosquitoes live in the margins of pools and in reeds alongside clear water. Preventative measures include the draining or oiling of such water, dosage with quinine, the use of mosquito-netting at night and the wearing of long sleeves and trousers at dusk and at dawn.'

'Roll your sleeves down, Vera!'

Chapter 14

The Chindit Invasion

While the Fourteenth Army and the enemy were locked in battle in the Arakan, Vinegar Joe Stilwell and the NCAC were advancing south from Ledo, over the border range and down into Burma. Preparations – stockpiling materials and equipment, recruiting engineers, mustering and training battalions of infantry – had begun in 1942 but it took until the end of 1943 for the march to begin.

Stilwell was over the mountains by the New Year of 1944 and fighting his way down the tortuous Hukawng Valley, dragging the Ledo Road and a 4-inch oil pipeline behind him. Engineers built at a rate of a mile each day with bridges being thrown across rivers and gorges on average every three miles. Leading the advance were the American-trained Chinese divisions, soon joined by the American 5307 Composite Regiment. This force of mobile infantry, formed in autumn 1943 from American volunteers and led by Major General Frank Merrill, was popularly known as 'Merrill's Marauders'. The long-range penetration training of these Americans had been organised by Wingate. His Chindits were about to give the Marauders, and the whole of the NCAC advance, invaluable support, with a second expedition behind enemy lines.

The operation planned this time was not so much an expedition as an invasion – deep into Burma, aiming to straddle the Myitkyina to Indaw railway line. It was designed to confuse the Japanese, disrupt their LOC and weaken their resistance to the NCAC drive southwards. The advance force, together with heavy earth moving equipment, was to be flown, on the night of 5-6 March, over the mountains, in seventy towed gliders, to land in natural clearings north of the Irrawaddy and 200 miles behind enemy lines.

Most of the Chindit troops were British, together with Gurkhas and West Africans. There were also American engineers, whose task was to convert the jungle clearings into airstrips capable of taking follow up Dakotas with more troops and equipment, and pack animals. Wingate's plan was then to set up a series of strongholds, from which marauding patrols, supplied from the air, could wreak havoc in the enemy rear.

The assault was feasible only because the Allies had gained a large measure of superiority in the skies. Heavy bombers of the US Strategic Air Force were operating in the theatre, targeting JAAF bases in Siam. At the same time, American P-51 Mustangs, with long-range tanks and each carrying two 1,000lb bombs, were destroying their aircraft on the ground in Burma, and the Spitfires and Hurricanes of 221 and 224 Groups RAF were pouncing on any that ventured into the battle zones.

The operation had effectively got underway a month earlier, when Brigadier Bernard Fergusson, a veteran Column Commander of the First Expedition, began marching Wingate's 16 Brigade down the Naga Hills, protecting Stilwell's right flank. They were nearing the area mapped out for the main assault as the planned date approached. But on the evening of 5 March, a reconnaissance Spitfire landed with a photograph showing that one of the two primary landing clearings, the one codenamed 'Piccadilly', had been obstructed with tree trunks. The Allied Commanders were in a quandary – had the secrecy of the whole effort been compromised? They kept their nerve and the attack went in on the other strip, 'Broadway'.

As night approached, the Dakotas of the USAAF Number 1 Air Commando – led by Colonel Philip Cochran, and known to the troops as 'Cochran's Circus' – each towing two gliders, hauled themselves off the runway at Lalaghat and set course to climb over the 8,000-feet mountain barrier of the Chin Hills. Of the sixty-seven gliders that flew through the darkness, eleven, their towropes snapping, were forced to land before the border. Another nine came down on enemy territory and fifteen more had to return to base because of the congestion on the ground.

Thirty-two landed at Broadway.

They were not so much landings as semi-controlled crashes. A great deal of the earth moving equipment was lost in the mêlée, but the engineers and troops – 400 had safely landed, with thirty injured and twenty-three dead – immediately began levelling the strip to the 1,000 yards minimum the Dakotas needed. They managed it, and the very next night, fifty-five aircraft were able to fly in, bringing reinforcements and evacuating the wounded.

Over five days, with two more landing grounds opened, the Dakotas flew 500 sorties and the gliders seventy-eight, transporting some 9,000 troops, over 1,000 pack-animals and 250 tons of equipment and supplies, at a casualty cost of 121 men. The Chindits had been, in Wingate's words, 'inserted into the guts of the enemy'.

Peter Bray made his first sortie to Broadway on 7 March, the second night of the operation. It was to be one of many:

'We'd take off before dawn, loaded with supplies and troops, or with mules, horses or even oxen. These were separated in heavy cane pens. We brought out casualties – and on occasion exhausted Chindits. There wasn't much room between the jungle and the strip so we had to come in just above stalling speed, with full flap – hanging on the props so to speak – and drop her in. Take-off was much the same – get her off early, straight and level to build up speed and then coax her over the trees. At first it was a rough old landing run, but the engineers kept at it – filling in the water buffalo holes and cutting down trees – and before long even Spitfires could get in and out. It was well before the full monsoon but by the end of the month the weather deteriorated and, on the 25th, we met a wall of water and horrendous turbulence – it was one of the only times we couldn't get through.

'But by then we had worries other than just the Chindits on our minds. On 17 March, the Japs launched their attack across the Chindwin on Imphal and Kohima, and we were at full stretch.'

It was only ten days after the Chindits flew in that the enemy

'March on Delhi' began in earnest. Their assault through the Arakan, although delivered with the usual determination, was in effect designed as a feint to mask the main thrust through Manipur. The Japanese 15th Division besieged Tamu, a Fourteenth Army outpost in the Kabaw valley to the east of Imphal, from which the 20th Indian Division made a fighting retreat back to the main base. The enemy 33rd Division struck through Tiddim and attacked Imphal from the south, while the 31st circled round to the north and cut the Imphal to Kohima Road, the only supply road from the railhead at Dimapur. After only five days of the campaign, the Rising Sun was seen for the first time on Indian soil.

Had those attacks come two weeks earlier, the Chindit operation in the east would have been practically impossible, for the Dakotas would have been fully employed on other fronts. But the thirty odd Chindit columns had in fact been launched on their mission, and somehow they had to be supplied.

The weather was continuing to deteriorate and the pouring rain, low cloud and turbulence, together with the terrain, made sorties to the Chindits perilous in the extreme. On 24 March, Wingate himself was killed in an air crash, caught in a storm when flying to India to report.

Supply dropping flights could only be made because Allied air forces had established air superiority over the Japanese, but there was still anti-aircraft fire – slow moving Daks, at low level, made an easy target. Colin Lynch and his crew, on an air drop mission to Jessami on the last day of March, had a narrow escape:

'We circled the village several times while dropping, and it seemed deserted. But we were fired at on six occasions by enemy ack-ack and machine guns – and hit. On the sixth circuit, I set up one of the Vickers machine guns and strafed the Jap positions as we passed. Then we flew back to base for repairs.'

In the same month, Colin, promoted to flight sergeant in December the year before, completed his first tour of 500 hours and started on the second:

'On April Fool's day, we were detailed to take troops and freight to "Aberdeen", one of the Chindits' strongholds. We took off from Lalaghat at five in the afternoon, and flew through thunder, lightning and hail all the way.'

But even in the half light, the silver waters of the Chindwin and Irrawaddy gave the aircrews good fixes:

'When we got there it was dark and the strip was flooded. On landing, we overshot and ran into a rocky mound at the end, colliding with a crashed American Dak that had hit the same mound the previous night. Our Dak was wrecked – both wings broken, engines torn off and fuselage snapped in two. We were trapped in the aircraft until a rescue team arrived and got the wounded out.'

Aberdeen by this time was under siege from the enemy, and Colin and his crew were marooned in the middle of a major action:

'At two in the morning, as we were trying to get some sleep in the wreckage of the Dak, there was a scuffling out on the jungle edge, followed by shots – and there we were, on the end of a full-scale Jap attack. People were killed, on both sides, but somehow they missed us. The next day, no one from the squadron flew in because of the danger from enemy air attacks. It was not until the next night that the 'A' Flight Commander landed, and took us out.'

On 18 May, Peter Bray made his final sortie to the Chindits' area:

'When it was an air drop, it was a six-hour trip – you had to do up to a dozen circuits to get the stuff out. On this one, we flew out by day to drop Bren guns, rolls of barbed wire and ammunition at "Blackpool", a new strongpoint they'd set up thirty miles south-west of Mogaung, over the railway and not more than a score of miles from where the enemy were facing Stilwell's forces.

'The fellows we brought out had some stories to tell and we knew from our own RAF chaps with them on the ground what hardships the Chindits were facing, and how vital these air drops were for them. Poor blighters – soaked to the skin, bitten by leeches and hunted by Japs in that evil-smelling jungle. The food, letters from home, fags and ammo in our hold was manna for them. We also knew that they listened to us circling around above the mist or the cloud, and how dispiriting it was to hear us give up and fly away. So we took perhaps more risks than we should to get through.

'On this drop, the monsoon had got going at full blast, but we pressed on. The nav did damned well to find the place – fortunately we picked up the railway line and followed it. But the Japs had set up a lot of guns along it and we came under very heavy fire indeed.

'There was more around Blackpool, where the enemy had it under siege. We got in seven drops – the aircraft all over the place and bullets whistling past. Then, through the windscreen in the pouring rain I could see the smoke from shells exploding on the DZ itself. It was under attack. Our chaps couldn't get out to the packs we'd dropped and there was a real chance the Japs would get them. That was always a risk with air drops – the white chutes were a magnet for the enemy. So the ground controller sent up a red Very light, terminating the drop.

'We didn't push our luck any further. It was throttles open, flaps up, and back through the downpours to base – in the pitch black, of course.'

For three months, under their new leader, Brigadier Lentaigne, the Chindits blocked the railway to Myitkyina, the main Japanese base in northern Burma. They seriously disrupted the enemy's ability to bring up supplies and reinforcements and eased the path of Stilwell's liberators from the north. They also showed again that it was possible to meet and beat the Japanese in combat, and that major offensive operations could be sustained by air supply.

Meanwhile, over in the north-west, defensive operations were in need of the Dakotas. The front was ablaze.

Chapter 15

The Sieges of Imphal and Kohima

The main Fourteenth Army forward stronghold at Imphal stood at 3,000 feet in the middle of a pear-shaped plain of 600 square miles, east of the Manipur Mountains which wall off India from Burma. It housed a considerable army and airbase, with depots, dumps, administrative outfits, hospitals, and camps for native labourers in their thousands. These had toiled to construct two transport airfields and four fighter strips. Outposts were positioned on the only two roads leading out of the base, sixty miles north to Kohima and 167 miles south to Tiddim.

John Hart reached RAF Imphal, in February 1944:

'We were billeted in top-class bashas – eighteen blokes to a hut – with rattan screens in the windows to keep the beasties out. There was an Indian bearer for every six men. We called ours Lofty because he was – and a proud man too. He'd every right to be, as he'd been an infantry sergeant in France in the first lot. Now here he was, doing our dhobi every day, and we paid him just five rupees a week – that's not much more than half a dollar.

'The purified water tasted a bit bitter but the food was pretty good, and there was enough of it. We had a cigarette ration of fifty Players a month – because I didn't smoke I could trade 'em in for chocolate and such. There was a bathhouse with those petrol drum showers, and we had to keep ourselves smart – we didn't mind that, and the discipline was reassuring, like. We all got detailed for cookhouse duties – all for one and one for all, and all that.

'You were lucky if you didn't get prickly heat. That was

very painful – red hot needles, it was. Then, once the rash got you, in the groin or over the shoulders, it was hard to get rid of, and often turned septic. If the ointments didn't work you got sent away for a spell at a hill station, for the cooler air. A lot of lads got badly sunburnt, too – self inflicted injury that was, and a chargeable offence.

'I was allocated to 194 Squadron, loading and unloading the air supply Dakotas. We were supervised mostly by the Flight Sergeant Air Quartermaster and the pilot, who had to make sure all the stuff was in the right order, and in the right place in the aircraft so that it could fly properly. It was bloomin' hot work – in the middle of the day it was over 100 degrees in the shade. We unloaded all the supply stuff for the Imphal squadrons – ammo, petrol and spares – and loaded whatever they were dropping to the poor blighters out in the jungle. That could be anything, from bullets and shells, beer and bully, Jeeps and trailers – to bleedin' mules.

'Fantastic animals of course, mules. They told us they were the trucks of the jungle, so to speak. But they were buggers to get up the ramps, and when you'd manhandled them inside, they didn't like going into those bamboo pens. Now, your mule has the unique ability among four-legged beasts that as well as being liable to kick viciously backwards with its rear legs it can just as likely do the same forwards, with its front. They put a lot of dents in the fuselage skin – and in your shins too. A couple of Dak flights had to be abandoned when mules broke out of their pens and went haywire in the back.'

Within a month of John's arrival however, it was not just the heat and the mules which were a threat to his health. In the middle of March, 100,000 Japanese crossed the Chindwin, not much more than fifty miles from the Imphal base. The Fourteenth Army Commander had been expecting an attack and had already planned to withdraw his troops from the mountainous frontier into the plain, and fight the enemy where his garrisons and squadrons could stand their ground and be supplied by air. The Japanese had no air transport and with their LOC overstretched, as was happening in the Arakan, they should be vulnerable and ultimately beatable.

Such plans were feasible because by this time, the Allies had clear air superiority over the Imphal Plain, thanks to the efforts of the fighters of 221 Group. Operating out of the airfields of Imphal were three Spitfire and four Hurricane Squadrons, plus a Beaufighter detachment, together with the anti-aircraft batteries of the RAF Regiment. This force had, in the three months around Christmas 1943, destroyed sixty Oscars and Dinahs and damaged fifty more. American long-range Lightnings and Mustangs had then attacked the remaining Japanese aircraft on their forward airstrips.

As three Japanese divisions swept into the outlying valleys, the 17th Indian Division fought its way back from Tiddim to Imphal and the 20th Indian climbed the fifty miles of steep mountain tracks up from Tamu, hauling its vehicles out of the mud with elephants. The 23rd Indian Division and the 50 Parachute Brigade dug in at Ukhrul, forty miles north-east of the plain, where they delayed the enemy thrust from that direction for a valuable ten days, before making a fighting retreat to Imphal. The base was now under siege – it was not to be lifted for eighty days.

The invaders swept round Kohima, and that base too, was besieged. Five days after crossing the Chindwin, they could look down into Assam. But as Bill Slim had foreseen, the enemy again relied on speed and encirclement, carried minimum supplies and outran their LOC. The Allies, supplied from the air, stood their ground. The enemy attack was held.

Air supply was in operation from the very start. The Dakotas dropped mail and newspapers to the divisions on the withdrawal to Imphal, and evacuated the wounded to hospitals in Dimapur and Comilla as soon as they struggled into base – both efforts a major boost to morale. The transports had, for several weeks, been flying out from the plain all non-combatants and civilians, a total of 52,000, and replacing them with fighting men, flown in over the heads of the enemy.

Nevertheless, the defence of this key base was a close run thing. The Japanese attacks were ferocious and for the first time in weeks, their fighter formations got through to support their troops. John Hart found himself in the firing line:

'Anyone who could hold a rifle had one, but mine didn't get fired – more's the pity. The base seemed to be well protected. The RAF Regiment got themselves dug in all round and not a single Jap got through that we could see. But they shelled us all right, especially when they managed to get themselves up on top of the hills to the north. And there were Oscars shooting us up – we spent a lot of time jumping into bunkers right alongside the aircraft dispersals. We knew pretty well what was going on from the radio, but I suppose they only gave the good news. Come to think of it, it was all pretty much good news – we were holding out. We got a bit short on food – 75 per cent rations, we were on – but we survived. In the end, the main danger for us ground crew was from the bloomin' mosquitoes!'

The air threat to John and his mates was seen off early in the siege. The Allies' 3rd Tactical Air Force swept the Oscars from the skies, and then set to strafing and bombing in close support of the defending troops. There was danger to the Spitfires and Hurricanes from enemy shelling but this risk was minimised by the fighters flying out to neighbouring airbases at night and back for operations at dawn the next morning.

Throughout the siege, the airstrips at Imphal were kept open, and transport aircraft poured in supplies to the beleaguered defenders. A score or more sorties to the base in April and May, are listed in Peter Bray's logbook:

'There were still some drops to be done at Jessami and other outposts, but mostly, we'd land at Imphal Main. It was still hazardous, the dangers being from ground fire, and the shelling of course, and the weather. On the way in we had to watch the air currents set up by the pre-monsoon winds over the mountains. Then, over the plain, the dust clouds meant you couldn't see much more than a mile in front of you. Early on, you had to keep a good lookout for Jap sneak fighters coming at you out of the murk.

'When they'd been chased away, there was the ground fire. The Japs were so close to the landing strips that you could see them looking up at you with their machine guns spraying bullets. You had to hold your nerve. But then, we had a nice comfortable base in Assam to go back to. Those squaddies, and our ground crew, had to stay there in the trenches, and get behind a rifle barrel at night.

'Also, it got a bit dicey with all the aircraft buzzing around – until a couple of air corridors were set up. That did the trick. They got the rate up to 300 supply planes into and out of Imphal each day. As well as keeping the defenders going, some 30,000 casualties were flown out. What a show it all was... Mind you, it was worse up at Kohima.'

The crack Japanese 31st Division had crossed the Chindwin further north, at Homalin, and advanced across the border into the Somra Hills, heading for Kohima. General Slim had expected the Japanese to come that way, as the hill station was the last Allied stronghold before the enemy's ultimate objective, the Bengal-Assam railhead at Dimapur, just forty-two miles away. The garrison had therefore been reinforced and new defences dug, but the attack came sooner, and in greater strength, than the Allied commanders had expected.

As the enemy swept forward, defending the stronghold, on a saddle at 5,000 feet, were mixed units of the Gurkhas, Burma Regiment and various Indian regiments. Also in the town were administrative and transport units, and a hospital, in which 1,500 wounded were at risk. Further reinforcements were urgently required.

Mountbatten was in Ledo, in a hospital bed with a serious eye injury – he had come to grief when his Jeep ploughed through a bamboo clump on the Northern Front. His head swathed in bandages, he discharged himself and got to a wireless set. On his own initiative he ordered twenty-four American air transports (Curtiss Commandos with a passenger load double that of the Dakota) off the Hump Route to fly the 5th Indian Division up from the Arakan. By this means, part of the 161 Indian Infantry Brigade, headed by the Royal West Kents, was able to reach Kohima on 5 April – just before the town was completely encircled by the Japanese. The remainder of the brigade was likewise surrounded and cut off a few miles down the road back to Dimapur.

Kohima was then defended by no more than 3,500 men against 15,000 of the enemy for sixteen days and nights, holding the bridgehead to India.

Earlier, at the beginning of February when the Japanese thrust into the Arakan was beginning to falter, General Slim, already reckoning that extra defenders would be needed further north, ordered the 7th Indian Division, George Hufflett's outfit, to withdraw from the Tamu mountains:

> 'We hoofed it all the way back to Cox's Bazaar. It was quite a trek but at least we were walking away from the Japs – for a while anyway, we hoped. We'd been squaring up to them for two whole months – December and January – and really roughing it. We were glad of the break.
>
> 'We were trucked on to Chittagong and this great big airbase, crowded with Yankee bombers and all sorts. We got a bit of a rest – changed our rags for some new kit, had a proper shower, and a good meal or two. Then they said we were going flying, up to the border to reinforce the line. So they marched us off to a Dakota.
>
> 'It was my first flight – ever. I remember an RAF sergeant sorting us out into pairs of about the same height and size, saying he had to get weight distribution spot on, so that the aeroplane would fly right. Made me think a bit, that did. We clambered up inside and sat down leaning against the walls – weren't any seats or safety belts. Stank in that Dak, it did – mule-shit I reckon. Then the engines start – quite a nice steady noise – and before you know it, we're off.
>
> 'It wasn't half bumpy in that Dakota. A lot of the lads were sick, but not me – I was very grateful for that. I had to go to the lav though. We all did, and that wasn't very comfortable. There was this door at the rear of the cabin – you had to bend down to get through it and then you couldn't stand straight when you had. There was a sort of skylight on one side and

underneath it was this chemical toilet – a bit of a pong in there later on.

'After about a couple of hours droning away, we landed – Ledo, the sergeant said it was. Well, we taxied around for a bit, and then, blow me if we didn't take off again. They told us the pilot had taken us to the wrong place! Any road, in another hour, we got to the right place, Dimapur.'

For the rest of February, George was on patrol, first of all in the freight trucks of the Bengal-Assam railway:

'They chugged up and down the line, all of us poking our heads over the side with our rifles at the ready all set to sort out any Japs who might be nosing around. We didn't see any. But then, on April Fool's Day mind you, we were sent up to cover the hills west of the Kohima to Imphal road. We saw some then all right.

'There was all sorts of vegetation up in those hills, and any one of the clumps could have a Jap in it. We had Naga tribesmen fighting with us. Bigger than your normal natives they were – good blokes. Bloomin' cold it was up there in the mountains, especially at the end of the month when the monsoon started. We were dug into foxholes and had to keep bailing 'em out with mess tins. But don't try and tell me about steaming hot tropical rain. Up there at night, the bottoms of our trouser legs froze stiff. Rough, it was – and there were Japs everywhere.'

By 4 April, Tokyo Radio was claiming, prematurely, that Kohima had fallen, and Imphal into the bargain. The Japanese propaganda machine had expected that the usual tactic of surprise and encirclement would lead to a quick, decisive victory – but again the enemy High Command had forgotten the air.

To reinforce the defence of Dimapur, General Slim called for the 33rd Indian Corps HQ and the crack British 2nd Division, both on the other side of the subcontinent at the time, to get across to Dimapur at the double. In the 33rd Signals Headquarters was Signalman Ken Brown:

'The division was scattered all over south-west India, but I was in the barracks at Poona, with 3 Company, Number 58 Medium WT Section – IEF Signals for short. They'd seen action in the Western Desert, Sicily, Crete and Persia – overseas without home leave since 1940, poor blighters. We had four of these thirty-hundredweight Chevrolet trucks loaded up with American signals gear and towing half-ton trailers with 110 volt generators – big stuff. We were training to join the Indian Expeditionary Force for a scheduled seaborne invasion of the Andaman Islands, south of the Bay of Bengal.

'Then, one morning, I get summoned by the Company Sergeant Major. He says, "You ride a motorbike?" I say, "Not me, Sergeant Major"' He says, "I've seen you riding around the barracks – you do." Then I say, "I haven't got a licence." So he gets an official-looking form, stamps it and signs it. "Well, now you have – sign here." With the stroke of a pen, I'm a dispatch rider.

'All the units hightailed it back to Poona, and we set off in convoy across India – ninety-eight vehicles and two motor-bikes. Mine was a BSA 500cc M20 – lovely machine, only one puncture all the 2,260 miles to Dimapur. At a roundabout in Calcutta we met an American convoy – great big trucks they were and they reckoned they had right of way. But the Indian traffic cop stood his ground, and let us through first. The Yanks just had to wait while I counted through every one of our vehicles, and the other bike. At Alipore, they loaded everything onto flatbeds on the narrow gauge railway, while I rode ahead into Dimapur to tell Fourteenth Army HQ that the convoy was on the way.'

For a moment there, Ken was famous. General Slim was impressed with the speed of 2nd Division's arrival – they had got there in forty-eight hours, non-stop. They were immediately ordered up the Kohima road to clear it, link up with the isolated 161 Brigade – and relieve the siege:

'Only a quarter of the signals units had arrived, so I was plucked out of HQ, and sent up the road with a wireless set, in a Jeep. What a road that was – sheer cliffs on one side and a sheer drop on the other. We pass this sign saying, "Beyond This Point You Are In Sight Of The Enemy" and straight away a bullet rips right through the canvas roof of the Jeep, just above our heads. What a welcome!

'Me and two other blokes dig into a foxhole six-feet square. Right by us we had the 10th Field Regiment with their 25-pounders – boom, boom, boom all the time. I had one of the newer, smaller British wireless sets, for receiving and sending five-letter scrambled and coded messages to 2 Div HQ. I also had a Fullerphone, an RT machine which worked on telephone lines. The messages on that were in clear, so I was able to get a better picture of what was going on. Basically, 15,000 Japs were mounting a more or less continuous bombardment from the hill terraces pretty much all round Kohima, beating the shit out of the poor blighters under siege. Beats me how they managed to hold out.'

Hemmed into a narrow ring, and fighting hand-to-hand with Japanese soldiers crawling forward at night, they held out through extraordinary grit and determination – and air supply.

During the siege, Colin Lynch flew sorties to Kohima most days, and often twice a day:

'It was a three and a half hour round trip from Agatarla. It was easy to find. You could see the road from Dimapur snaking up the valley to the mountains and at the top, at 5,000 feet, there's the Kohima Ridge, not quite a mile long. Where the road turns right and runs along the ridge and off down to Imphal, there's a whole lot of hillocks, and in the middle of those you could see Kohima hill station – or what was left of it.

'On both sides of the ridge, the mountains rise up another thousand feet or so and that's where the Japs were, lobbing their shells and mortar bombs into our troops. We had to run the gauntlet to make a drop. There'd usually be a line of Daks going in, one after the other. We dropped them everything you could think of – but mostly ammo, rations and medical supplies. And after the monsoon started we dropped them a load of tarpaulins so they could catch some water. There wasn't much of a DZ even from the start, and as the siege went on, we got down to dropping on what used to be the District Commissioner's tennis court. By then, there wasn't anything much of the place left standing. The trees had all been blasted and were smothered in white parachutes.'

Peter Bray made more than a dozen drops to the besieged troops:

'The ghastly thing was that we could see it all as we went in on our runs. There were our lads, dug in just a shovel's length from the Jap trenches. Dead bodies lying all around, and wounded crawling back from no man's land. And there'd been a hospital there – horrible. What those men suffered doesn't bear thinking about. I'd never before seen anything so dreadful and I'd never want to see such things again.'

The ruined hospital was in the vicious hands of the Japanese, so the British and Indian medics had fallen back to an Advanced Dressing Station, where they worked miracles, despite being under fire from snipers and taking three direct shell bursts. Wounded men were patched up, went back into battle and were wounded again, three or four times. The surgeons performed amputations with a knife. One of the doctors, a Colonel Young, crawled through enemy lines to tend the wounded.

Meanwhile, the 2nd Division was pressing up the road from Dimapur, itself supplied from the air. Peter remembered:

'It was tricky making the drops on that road. As well as the hills and the blinding rain, the slopes above and below the road were at forty-five degrees. The only way we could get the ammo in was to drop it practically slap-bang into the gun pits.'

The Japanese launched their shells, snipers and infantry with no lesser ferocity on the relieving forces. The first reinforcements to reach the mayhem at Kohima hellhole made it by crawling up a gulley that led through enemy defences. That was on 18 April, nearly three weeks after the village had been surrounded. That gully approach was widened to a wedge and the Camerons and Worcesters cleared a path for ambulances to go in – they were shelled in their turn. Then, on the 19th, the Royal Berkshire Regiment marched in and raised the siege.

But the battle was far from finished. The enemy had to be cleared from the heights above the town before Kohima could be considered relieved. More troops took the road up there for that task, including the 1st Queen's and George Hufflett:

'We went up part of the way in trucks and then on foot – on that road we felt safer on our own two feet. We got dug in alongside a regiment of Gurkhas. There were Japs and bullets everywhere. I was several nights at one end of this old tennis court, with Japs at the other calling over to us, "What's the time, Tommy?" One of our blokes took a bullet in the jaw, and after a time it turned septic and got all maggoty. He reckoned those maggots saved his life. Then they went for an all-out effort to take the place. Came at us like demons, they did – but we kept 'em out. One of our blokes claimed he'd cut down over forty of the blighters with one burst of his tommy gun.'

The central position in the heights held by the enemy, was the 7,000-feet Jail Hill:

'The artillery had given it a right old pasting – second only to Alamein they reckon it was. But the lads who made the first frontal attack got driven back, so at the crack of dawn on the 8 May, it's our turn.

'I've got hold of a tommy gun, which steadies the nerves a bit, but that old hill's bloomin' steep and there's not much cover on it. And the top's a long way off. Anyway, our gunners lay down a barrage of smoke, and off we start up the slope. Covering fire and movement – we know the drill pretty well by now. After about an hour we've bagged a good number of Japs and got a fair old way up. Then it all gets a bit confused.

'There's this machine gun set up about thirty yards away, and giving us merry hell. So the sergeant shouts out for us to dig in. To get the shovel out I'm lifting up my arm like this – and the Jap gets me with a burst of his bloody bullets. I suppose I must have yelled, and rolled down the hill a bit – and then I passed out.'

George had taken three bullets in the right forearm. They came in at the elbow and took out the nerves and artery in the forearm. The muscles were hanging like meat from the bone, and he was losing blood fast:

'The lads got me to a field dressing station – just a shelter really, there was no water. They patched me up a bit. It didn't half hurt, my arm, but there was a Gurkha there who'd been shot in the face – he was a lot worse off than me. They gave me a shot of morphine and next thing I knew I was in the back of an ambulance, bucketing down the mountain. I reckoned the battle would have to go on without me.'

Back on Jail Hill, the 1st Queen's had managed to dig in. They exchanged fire with the Japanese all that day, and through the night, when two companies of Gurkhas got up in support. The next day George's mates advanced a bit further, and then there was a third night of it before, on the fourth day, the enemy were driven out from their bunkers. It was a key moment in the battle.

At the height of the Kohima action, Vera Lynn reached Dimapur, twelve miles down the road from the siege. There she met the war correspondent Dicky Sharp who, scenting a good story and a few dramatic pictures, asked her if she was willing to go up the road to the frontline. She said she was, but the Army forbade it – too dangerous for her and too much responsibility for them.

But she was tireless in her efforts to entertain the boys brought down the road from Kohima and flown in from Imphal to be patched up, operated on, and too often, to die, in the base hospitals of Dimapur. She sat at the foot of beds in the tented wards, smiled, signed autographs, got the occasional kiss – and sang her songs.

Vera wasn't the cause of homesickness among the boys in the Arakan, Imphal and Kohima. What she brought was a reminder of their wives and sweethearts at home and a reassurance that they weren't forgotten. She had come all the way out there to see them – and they loved her.

Chapter 16

Two Casevacs

The Queen Alexandra's nurses in Dimapur were used to seeing blood and gore and didn't turn a hair at the state of George Hufflett's arm – but they might just have raised an eyebrow on noticing that underneath his blanket, he was starkers:

'I was a bit dizzy from the sedative when I got to that hospital. I'd been asleep on a stretcher – lovely dreams of the South Downs. It was a rude awakening when they came to mess about with my arm. They'd taken everything I had – weapons, boots, clothes, the lot. I suppose they needed them for other blokes still fighting – but I was mad as hell I'd lost my brand new pullover. And what about my pay book, and my identity tag? I had nothing, and was nobody. By this time my arm was giving me real gyp, and I started to feel sorry for myself, and very lonely. Then they gave me another jab, and I dozed off again.

'It was all hazy from then on. They must have operated because once when I came to, I found my arm was all plastered up. Then later on I found that some caring soul had restored my modesty a bit – with a pair of blue football shorts!

'I don't know how long it was before I sat up and looked around. We were in a sort of tented ward, with wounded blokes all round. The nurses were bloomin' marvellous – worked their socks off and always had a smile. A medic came and told me about those Jap bullets in my arm – they'd got them out, but they'd have to send me off for special treatment. He talked about a skin graft. It was then I realised

I wouldn't be going back to the regiment any too soon, and that I probably had a Blighty one.'

George was transferred by train to a hospital boat on the Ganges:

'That was all right, that was. There was this lovely Indian nurse and if I asked really nicely she'd give me something to knock me out – I must have slept most of that trip. I do remember waking up at Benares, and seeing hundreds of Indians bathing in the river. And you couldn't miss the old Himalayas up there to the north.

'It wasn't until we got to Bareilly that somebody found me a pair of khaki trousers – a bit long they were, but more comfortable than the football shorts, and more dignified. They also gave me an emergency pay book, and ten rupees pay. I went and spent eight of 'em straight off, getting the trousers shortened. The other two paid what I owed the char wallah, and that was that.

'After a while, they took me and a bunch of walking wounded off the boat. We all got into ambulances and drove up this mountain road to Ranikhet hill station, where there was a hospital called the British and Indian General. Great big place it was, all among trees and with smashing views over the mountains. Lovely and cool – and peaceful.

'We're signed in by this young Indian doctor – he looks me up and down, makes a few notes, then sends me off to find this particular ward. So off I go, with a chit in my left hand, and my right hand and arm in plaster. Now, that plaster's getting a bit the worse for wear. I've been thinking for some time that perhaps my wound's gone bad – throbbing fit to bust, and muck coming out at both ends. Anyway, after wandering around for a bit, I find the right ward, where this fierce looking Irish nurse says, "You're not coming into my ward with that – go and get it cleaned up." So I hoof it all the way back to the first medic I saw, and he takes the plaster off and cleans it up. It didn't half sting – they had to give me another sedative after that.'

When the wound had sufficiently healed, surgeons carried out a graft, with skin from George's thigh:

'I must have been a couple of months in that hospital. I used to have fun teasing the Indians a bit. The nurses were ready for a bit of a laugh but once, I got into trouble with the caste system. I'd stuck the orderly's hat on the tea boy's head – and it turned out the orderly was an untouchable. Another thing I remember was that there were scores of these monkeys round the place – they gave us all a load of bother, pinching stuff.

'Anyway, in August, they wheel a bunch of us down the road and load us on one of those rackety old trains. Not a comfortable journey that one, but we fetched up in another hospital, in Poona. Then in September, they put us on a nice, clean New Zealand hospital ship, the *Rangitata*. We sailed on my twenty-first birthday – homeward-bound at last.'

In the same month that George was cut down, Ken Brown had begun to suffer from a splitting headache:

'We were in Kohima by this time. When I got up there and saw it, I couldn't for the life of me see how anyone could possibly have survived in that hellhole. Every basha and bungalow had been blown away, and the trees were just stumps, with shredded white parachutes still hanging there. I thought, They'll give out a few medals for this lot. There was still a lot to do to clear the Japs out of the hills all round, and the minefields they'd laid didn't make that any easier.

'Anyhow, I was getting a bit cross-eyed by now with the headache so I staggered over to the field station, reckoning I'd probably got malaria. The medic thought so too and put me in a tent where there were camp beds and a lot of mepacrine. Ten days I was there, being dosed with the stuff – and another drug but I never found out what that was. I didn't get any better – in fact I turned yellow. Another doctor diagnosed jaundice – and he'd got it right.

'I was moved down the hill to a casualty clearing station – where I got very ill. I was all of four months in various hospitals – one of them was a paddle-driven hospital ship on the Ganges. It was all very debilitating and I drifted in and out of consciousness for weeks – but I must have been *compos mentis* on 6 June, because we had this smuggled battery receiver and I heard the news of the Normandy landings.

'They took me up to Dehra Dun in the hills for convalescence. It was a fair old while before I was fighting fit again and it wasn't until December that I finally got back to the Signals.'

Chapter 17

Counterattack

Down in the Arakan, back in mid-February 1944, the Japanese invaders of Burma had found themselves for the first time on the back foot. Allied troops had not turned and fled, they had stood their ground and given as good as they got, and better. Seven days it was supposed to have taken for the enemy troops to get to Chittagong, and seven days' rations had been issued. But their timetable for the 'March on Delhi' was in tatters and they were starving, short of ammunition, and faced with fresh Allied divisions arriving from the north. One of those was the 36th British, within whose ranks was Private Henry Stock, in his signals platoon:

'They called us the "Doh Ring Div" – our shoulder-flashes sported these two linked rings, white and red, and doh was Urdu for two. We advanced down the west side of the Mayu Range, about the first in '44 after Stilwell to go on the offensive against the Japs.

'The Gurkhas and the Punjabis came down the spine of the mountains. Bloody brave that was – we could see it was like a razor edge up there. They pushed the enemy down towards us where they were trapped. Our blokes in the Boxes over to the east killed thousands of them. Those they couldn't shoot, the RAF bombed and strafed, and when they had to go back to refuel, the artillery and the tanks took over. We now knew for sure that we could stand up to the Japs in the field, and beat them. We couldn't wait to get after them, and finish them off.'

And get after them they did. On the eastern side of the range, Allied tanks and infantry, which had stormed the Okeydoke Pass, pressed on down the valley where the fortified Boxes now blocked the Japanese withdrawal. The Admin Box was relieved on 23 February.

Most of the air transports were busy further north but supplies to all the divisions in the Arakan could now come in up the Naf River – cleared with the help of the Royal Navy – now back in the Bay of Bengal – and over the mountain passes. The West Africans had worked wonders in the Kaladan Valley to the east, not only protecting the flank by killing 1,500 of the enemy and capturing one of their airfields, but also building a seventy-five mile supply road through the jungle. They were now brought in to the eastern bank of the Mayu River, getting there after a five day forced march through the jungle.

In the first week of March, Henry and his comrades in arms pushed further south:

'The Japs had set up this enormous fortress at Razabil. Dug in thirty feet or more under the hills, they were, and fighting tooth and nail. But our gunners launched a barrage against them, and when they let up, the tanks advanced, guns blazing. All day it went on. Then, after nightfall, our blokes went in with bayonets and got the blighters out.

'Then we had a go at those tunnels, at the western end. The Japs weren't giving up easily here either, but a tank from the Welsh battalion came up trumps – got a shell into the tunnel mouth, and blew up the ammo dump. Went up like a good 'un, that did. In the confusion the Taffs rushed in and the defenders were done for. And apart from clearing out nests of Nips – a lot of them committed suicide – that was that. The western end of the tunnels was ours.'

The tanks and infantry took the eastern end in April, but the struggle to hold the line was far from over. The enemy brought up reinforcements and aircraft and counterattacked in their turn, in concert with their attacks in the north. They were beaten by the mud of the monsoon, which started at the end of the month, the endurance of the Allied soldiers, and by the fighters that continued to operate from all weather strips. Between the turn of the year and 15 May, the RAF's Spitfires and Hurricanes claimed 315 enemy aircraft destroyed, with another seventy probable, and 225 damaged.

The Second Battle of the Arakan had been won. The Japanese had lost close to 7,000 of their finest troops, killed or wounded. It was the first great victory of the Fourteenth Army. The Allied commanders now had a line to defend through the monsoon and malaria season. Stability was the key requirement on this front, while up in the north the NCAC pushed on down the Ledo Road, and on the Central Front, General Slim's divisions advanced to dislodge the enemy from the Manipur Range.

At Kohima, following the final assault on Jail Hill, Sappers of 2nd Division cleared the minefields along the ridge, enabling British tanks to rumble in. One by one the remaining half dozen Japanese strongholds fell and, by 14 May, after fifty days and nights of struggle, Kohima Ridge was back in Allied hands. In the battle, the enemy had lost 4,000 dead.

At Imphal, by the end of May the Japanese had been beaten back, and were trapped in their bunkers. Meanwhile, the Allies broke out from Kohima, and fought their way south, reopening the road to Imphal on 22 June. The fate of the Japanese invasion of India was sealed. All had been staked on capturing the food, ammunition and transport at Allied bases and now, in retreat, they faced starvation. There was no air supply to come to their aid.

The tide had turned in the Burma campaign. The Allies had held the line and won the day.

All four RAF Dakota squadrons were now operational, flying through the monsoon in close support of the advancing troops, from the Tiddim road in the south, up to Kohima in the north. The action up there still demanded regular air drops as the capacity of the switchback road from Dimapur was outstripped by the needs of Allied garrisons.

Wide-ranging operations were being mounted against the struggling Japanese divisions. In one such, south-east of Imphal, the Lushai Brigade (three Indian, and the Chin Hills battalions) outflanked the retreating enemy, cutting off their line of escape down the Tiddim road. In this outstanding action, the Lushai troops were supplied entirely by air drop, the Dakota crews making good their deliveries in the tight mountain valleys, despite the cloud and rain.

American transports were in the action too, including Number 3 Combat Cargo Task Force (CCTF) of the USAAF, with their C-47s. Now serving in that unit was the RAF's Aircraftman Richard Hull:

'I arrived at Imphal in mid-'44, for assignment to the fighter ops room, where they controlled the Hurricanes flying off down the hill valleys. But the Commanding Officer said, "Go and work with the Yanks at Tulihal, they're short of blokes." So I went.

'Tulihal had an enormous runway 6,000 yards long and 150 yards wide. They said that the Yanks' measurement specifications had been misunderstood by the Brits who were building it. Should have been feet, not yards. The runway was made with "bithess" – hessian covered in bitumen – which was pretty durable but like a sponge when it got wet. Evidently there used to be a considerable hill at one end but the Yanks levelled it with two gigantic bulldozers which just drove round and round in circles until it was flat.

'The airmen's quarters were wattle and mud daub bashas with thatched roofs. I found a four foot long green snake under my bed and this Yank said, "Don't worry about them, they're harmless – it's the little kraits in your boots you want to look out for!" I was nervous of my boots from then on. But the termites were the worst – they'd eat the leather off your water bottle in one night. We had good American rations – we Brits sometimes swapped our bully beef for extra spam. The Yanks liked our bully – they used to smother it in tomato sauce. We preferred spam, and McConochie's tins of curried meat and veg.

'There were Indian Air Force Vultee Vengeances on the base, and our nine C-47s. The aircrews had towed gliders for the Chindits. The Yanks had their ground crews organised differently from the RAF. One man was responsible for "the ship", as they called it – did the engineering, made sure it was in good order and passed it fit for flying. Then he went along on the flights as drop master.

'I was allocated straight away to aircrew dispatch duties – dropping all kinds of supplies to the troops fighting their way through Tiddim, Tamu and Kennedy Peak and so on. Sorties were forty-five minutes each way plus half an hour for dropping, to units miles from anywhere. I can still see one bunch of troops perched on top of a mountain with the 25-pounder gun they'd dragged up with a fifteen hundred-weight Chevvy truck. The chutes from the drops were draped all over the trees. There was one bloke waving from the truck – then he had to duck away sharpish when a pack of bully beef cans broke up in the air. It struck me that that lot had probably been marooned in the jungle on that hill for days, being got at by the Japs, and all they had to look forward to was advancing or retreating to another one. We, on the other hand, would fly back to base and all its relative comforts. That was the way of it.

'But we didn't have it all easy. In the worst of monsoon weather, it wasn't the most comfortable place to be, by that door; rain soaked everything in reach and made manhandling the packs tricky. It was difficult to do much other than hang on tight, watch your step, and push. Once, I took out my precious Conway Stewart fountain pen to make a note of something or other, and lost it over the sill – stupid really. And another time we had a pack hang up – beat itself to death against the fuselage and the webbing split. This chunky American drop master whipped out his machete and chopped the whole lot away. Off it went – only just missed the tailplane.

'It got chilly in those clouds, with just our tropical kit on. I used to go up front with the pilots to warm up. They found out I was useful with wireless and radios and got me to help out with those. They had RCA radios, good for RT, and a radio compass. Tulihal had a good strong beacon for getting a steer back to base.

'I enjoyed those few months with the Yanks, but then they

were recalled to China and I got posted to Quetta – for Wireless Operator Mechanic Group One training.'

Added to the morale boosting air drops was the humane service rendered by air evacuation. The practice of lifting wounded from jungle clearings had been initiated by the RAF in the First Arakan advance of 1943, with modified Tiger Moths and Fox Moths. The difficulty of evacuating wounded from the First Chindit Expedition in 1943 had led Mountbatten to propose, at the Quebec Conference, that a light air ambulance service be set up. The idea was adopted and American Stinson L-1 Vigilant and L-5 Sentinel single engined high wing monoplanes had come into service in the American Air Commando Group. Operating in and out of rough strips often not more than about 300 yards long and 30 yards wide, they rescued hundreds of Allied casualties from the jungle in the Second Chindit Expedition in 1944, and continued throughout the campaign. American pilots were joined by RAF personnel, aircrew and medical orderlies.

Numbers of wounded Chindits were flown out from jungle strips by the Dakotas. Many of those landings and take-offs were dramatic enough, but the Americans had developed an even more spectacular method for getting the boys out – the Glider Pickup. This was used from early in the NCAC campaign, and the British Dakota squadrons took it up in due course. Norman Currell explains the procedure:

'When a message came in that there had been a number of casualties on a battlefield, we'd either tow a glider over, or use one already there. The chaps on the ground would turn it into any wind there was, and load the casevacs on board. In the meantime, the Pickup Station would have been set up – two poles, ten feet long and twenty feet apart. A loop of nylon hawser would be fastened to a hook on the nose of the glider and strung across the tops of the poles.

'The glider "pickup" Dakota was fitted with a seventeen foot boom which could be lowered by a crew member newly acquired for the purpose. We called him the engineer. Along this boom ran a wire cable with a heavy hook attached at the end. The other end of the cable was attached to a winch which was bolted under the central mainplane.

'We'd circle overhead – machine guns mounted, watching out for fighters – waiting for the signal that all was ready. Then we'd come in at 1,000 feet into the wind, lower the boom and throttle back for a dive to 140 miles per hour. We'd swoop in at twenty-five feet or so over the glider. Exciting stuff. The drill was that the hook would then grab the hawser, taking up the slack. The hook would then come off the boom and pay out for two seconds. Then, after another three seconds an automatic brake would stop the cable running out. After that it was, "Full Throttle" and hey presto, if all went well the glider was picked up – having accelerated from zero to a 105 miles per hour in five seconds!

'The initial test was to pick up a glider loaded with 18,000lbs of cement! I can still remember the ear-splitting, grinding shriek when the automatic brake grabbed the cable – and the stink from the burning clutch plates! It was worse than anything I had previously experienced. We weren't permitted to land for a whole hour so that the whole thing could cool off.

'In operation it was a tricky manoeuvre but if all went well, and it usually did, the glider and its occupants were on their way to the nearest medical station. It was well worth the risks.'

Other aircraft braved the Japanese fighters to get the wounded out. In June '44, the aircrews of 31 Squadron Dakotas flew a series of missions to air drop on the shores of Lake Indawgyi. It was a long way over to the east, deep in Chindit country. In anything like decent weather it was not difficult to spot – the only sizeable lake in northern Burma, at the end of a tributary of the Irrawaddy. At dropping height over the lake, they were taken aback on one occasion to see two Sunderland flying boats, parked out on the water. How on earth did they get there? Of course, they had to have been flown in. But they were miles from the nearest sea base. And what were they there for?

Back at Agartala, they discovered that those Sunderlands, which had been designed for submarine patrol work, had been stripped of their armament, and flown to one of the wider stretches of the Brahmaputra in northern Assam. Then – the world's largest aircraft at the time – they skimmed over the mountains and down the valleys of the wildest parts of Burma, to put down on Indawgwi. It was, to say the least, an impressive feat of airmanship. The aircrew took the risk in order to evacuate over 600 sick and wounded Chindits, before bad weather and rough water stopped the operation on 11 June. The troops nicknamed the flying boats 'Gert and Daisy'.

There was no one among the Allied commanders who knew better the value of air supply than Bill Slim, but he also knew that it was limited in availability, and expensive in resources, and that major movements in the jungles of Burma, for both sides, were still dependent on rivers and roads. To drive the Japanese south to Mandalay, there had to be a supply road in north Burma – the highway that General Stilwell's NCAC was pushing through the valleys from Ledo.

Now under Slim's direct command, on 19 March, his sixty-first birthday, Stilwell crossed the pass between the Hukawng and Mogaung Valleys and by June, his American-trained Chinese forces were pressing on the railway that the Chindits were disrupting from the south, and within striking distance of the town of Mogaung itself. Meanwhile, Merrill's Marauders, who had started their march south from Ledo in February, were making a flanking move to the left, striking out for Myitkyina, the key eastern Burma town and airfield that had fallen to the invaders in May 1942.

On their advance, the Marauders (three battalions of 400 men each) were supplied from the air by 2nd Troop Carrier Squadron USAAF, which dropped an average of 15 tons each day. Guided by Kachin tribesmen, after a forced march of twenty days, they scaled the 7,000 foot Nauri Hykit Pass and, on 17 May, launched a sudden attack on the Myitkyina airstrip, where they became isolated. But just five hours after their unexpected arrival, Troop Carrier Command came to their rescue, with glider loads of engineers and equipment, followed by Dakotas with supplies and reinforcements, including a troop of

British anti-aircraft gunners. Bill Old was once more in the van, closely followed by Vinegar Joe himself.

Down the railway to the west, the Chindits stormed Mogaung, cut the railway and linked up with Stilwell's Chinese. The Japanese defenders of Myitkyina fought fanatically and there followed an eleven-week struggle to take the town. Throughout June and July, most, but not all the airfield was in Allied hands. Straight away, the two RAF Dakota squadrons, 31 and 194, now based at Agartala, began supply missions, by night and by day, to the besieged town.

It took five hours for the round trip. Depending on the weather – occasionally it was reasonable, even at the height of the monsoon – there'd be no difficulty finding it, about 200 miles east of Imphal. Past the Indawgyi Lake, the river and railway led straight to it – and if those were missed, the pilots could follow the other Dakotas flying in. The aircraft would form up, circling around a prominent peak out to the west, and then, more often than not with fighter escort, fly in a stream down an air corridor, running the gauntlet of enemy fire.

On the ground it was mayhem. The monsoon was going strong and the airfield was a sea of mud. It took up to an hour to turn the Dakota round, and with enemy lines no more than 3,000 yards away, the dispersals were often under shellfire. From time to time, Oscars would manage to get in at low level for a strafing run. Nevertheless, the aircraft delivered men, guns, ammunition and rations – and brought out as many wounded as could be carried.

Colin Lynch remembers taking out refugees:

'With the fighting going back and forth, there were plenty of them, suddenly cut off by a Jap surge – Burmese, Indians and Brits, all desperate to get out of the town. At times there were so many struggling to get on we'd have to manhandle them off the steps or we wouldn't have got away at all. As it was, overloaded, and perhaps damaged by Jap shellfire, it could be a struggle to make cruising height.

'We flew out along another air corridor, but again, we'd all mill about a bit to try and avoid the Jap guns. Once, in the confusion, some American aircrews broke RT silence, and six of their Daks got shot down. We got in and out every time, but once I was hit by shrapnel – bits of it are still in me to this day.'

Among the reinforcements brought in by the Dakotas was 36th British Division, flown up from the Arakan, and among their ranks was the Shiny 9th Battalion of the Royal Sussex, with Henry Stock:

'The hoo-ha started before we landed – there were ack-ack shells bursting all around us. It wasn't any safer on the ground – there was a right old battle going on. The Chinese, Chindits, Gurkhas and Yanks were so beaten up by weeks in the jungle, they looked like scarecrows. They had to put these orange-coloured ribbons on their hats and round their arms so they could tell who was, and who wasn't a Jap.

'We went straight into action. The odd Oscar fighter made a run over the base, but it was mostly our dive-bombers we saw, beating seven shades out of the Jap dugouts in the town. They fought like tigers – it was the flamethrowers that finally got them out.'

After seventy-eight days of siege, Myitkyina was regained by the Allies on 3 August. Nearly 4,000 Japanese perished. The key to the victory was the storming of Mogaung by the Chindits. With the railway cut off, the enemy were once again adrift from their LOC.

But the Chindits, who had been transferred to Stilwell's command for the attack, were neither trained nor equipped to be assault troops. They sustained heavy losses, not just from enemy action but also from disease and exhaustion. They had been four months in the jungle, in continuous combat. The remnants were flown out and the exploits of this charismatic force were over.

At a cost of 6,000 Allied, and 21,000 Japanese dead, the Ledo Road, and the valuable oil pipeline, had made it to Myitkyina. The airfield provided an advanced bomber base and was soon to reopen as the staging post for flights to China, giving the aircrews relief from the dangerous Hump route to the north.

The enemy had been driven out of north-east Burma and supplies could now come down Stilwell's new road.

On the Central Front, the Fourteenth Army broke out from Imphal and Kohima in July and by mid-August had driven the Japanese army, apart from trapped and desperate stragglers, out of India. Far from marching into Assam in triumph, the would-be invaders found themselves in headlong retreat.

The air belonged to the Allies. Enemy fighters had been driven back to Rangoon – they were using forward airstrips only to refuel – and their heavy bombers to Bangkok. At the end of a 3,000-mile long LOC and with no air supply of their own, Japanese soldiers were short of ammunition and rations and broken in spirit. According to popular belief, they were able to go for days on a handful of rice. They were in fact starving.

In the battles of Imphal and Kohima the enemy had lost 50,000 dead. General Slim was now set on clearing them from the mountains and herding them into the central plains, where he looked to fight a decisive battle.

From 12 July, the Dakotas of 62 and 117 Squadron flew in to Agartala as 31 Squadron was withdrawn from the action for a long overdue break from combat. But it was a working break, as Peter Bray recalls:

'Following the hoped for victory in Burma, the next campaign was expected to be a combined operation to liberate Malaya and the Andaman Islands. So after a couple of weeks off in Agatarla, on 7 August we all piled into our aeroplanes and flew over to the other side of India. We were detailed for training in paratroop dropping at Chaklala.

'That was a very interesting few weeks. Paratroop dropping was straightforward for us up front – different for the chaps leaping out of the door. But the Dak was a jump friendly aircraft, with plenty of room underneath the tailplane. Our wireless operators were given the opportunity of taking the Jump Master's course, and all of them were up for it. They made one jump each on the final day, and no one was hurt.

Dakota ZA947 at RAF Coningsby. (*Author*)

The Dakota 'office'. (*Author*)

George Hufflett in 1942 – from the mislaid paybook. (*George Hufflett*)

Peter Bray, 'B' Flight Commmander 31 Squadron RAF. (*Peter Bray*)

Colin Lynch, one of the last Observers. (*Colin Lynch*)

Colin Lynch ready for action. (*Colin Lynch*)

Sepoys of Air Supply Corps packing the containers that... (*RAF Air Historical Branch*)

...Fg Off Larsen and crew carry from Agartala to... (*Colin Lynch*)

... the DZ at Tiddim, where... (*Colin Lynch*)

...the Dispatchers make the delivery. (*IWM CI601*)
The author acknowledges the permission granted by
The Trustees of The Imperial War Museum, London for the use of their photographs.

Sinzweya DZ in the 'Admin Box'. (*IWM CI602*)

Sepoys salvaging 'chutes. (*RAF Air Historical Branch*)

Loading 20mm light anti-aircraft gun. (*RAF Air Historical Branch*)

RAF Air Liaison team calls in air-drop to the Chindits. (*RAF Air Historical Branch*)

Chindit strip at Broadway, March 1944. (*IWM SE7937*)

Imphal Main Base looking north to Japanese
gun positions. (*IWM MH4168*)

Siege of Kohima, tennis court battleground. (*IWM IND3483*)

Signalman Ken Brown recuperating in Darjeeling. (*Ken Brown*)

Vera Lynn at Dimapur, in the hospital... (*Dame Vera Lynn*)

...with the nurses (*Dame Vera Lynn*)

...with British and African boys. (*Dame Vera Lynn*)

Arthur Watts in Far East rig.
(*Arthur Watts*)

Air-drop at Myitkyina, 1,000 yards from Japanese lines. (*IWM CBI35851*)

Stinson L-5 Sentinel takes casualty on board. (*RAF Air Historical Branch*)

Monsoon operations, Dakota in the Arakan .
(*IWM CI718*)

Maungdaw–Buthidaung road tunnel.
(*IWM IND3409*)

Advancing through paddy fields in central Burma. (*IWM SE142*)

Bren gun team in action. (*IWM SE2067*)

'Spirits were high after all that and we were able to grab a few days' leave and make a memorable trip up to the North-West Frontier and Darjeeling. Most of us hadn't seen a British Raj hill station before. We were able to relax in the hotels and tearooms, and the cool climate cured a lot of prickly heat. The Himalayas looked stupendous – I enjoyed that view more than the terrifying glimpses I'd had of them over the Hump.'

With the aim of linking up with Slim for that decisive battle on the Burmese plains, the NCAC forces pushed on down from Myitkyina and Mogaung. As early as August, 36th British Division had begun to fight its way down the mainline railway corridor from Mogaung, aiming for Naba Junction east of Indaw, 100 miles away. The division advanced at an average of two miles a day, for the next six months. The Royal Sussex Regiment was with them. Henry Stock takes up the story:

'It was raining cats and dogs every day – made it very dangerous underfoot. We lost some of our pack animals – sucked into mud holes. We had to watch our step in the swamps, too. The ground was firmer in the teak forests and then there was a railway embankment to follow. The American engineers and the REME blokes fixed up some of the wagons, and got some Jeeps fitted out with flanged wheels, so they could motor up and down the tracks – good for carrying equipment, and men sometimes.

'We weren't half pleased to see those Daks coming in with the supplies. It was my job to lay out the signals for their drops – big white sheets, in the shape of a letter "L" in the daytime and petrol flares at night. The stuff we got was either British Pacific Rations, or the Yanks' "K" Rations. The Pacific packs came in a tin eighteen inches square and six inches deep – they were the usual hardtack affairs and had to feed twenty-four men for a day. The "K" rations were something else – all kinds of bits and pieces they had, and coffee and fags too. Those with a "B" on the box were for breakfast, and they had a couple of sheets of toilet paper with them. "L" was for lunch and "D" for dinner – with those you could get a decent sized tin of half a chicken, or streaky bacon. We were always after those Yankee packs.

'Leeches and ticks were a nightmare, getting through our clothes and into our boots. Flies were at us during the day, and mozzies at night – and so were the Japs. We'd often call in support from the bombers to drop a stick or two on the blighters right in front of us. We had to have great faith in the bomb-aimers. The fighter-bombers too – they came ruddy close. You were all right with our boys in their "Hurribombers", Vengeances and Beaufighters, but you had to keep your head down with some of the Yanks.

'The worst of all the battles was down the corridor, at the railway depots of Pinwe. The Japs had their dugouts there in the woods, behind all these deep streams. The Chinese artillerymen were advancing with us, and they really came into their own then. But it still took three weeks to clear the Japs out – until the end of November. By the time we'd finished there wasn't much of the place left.

'I felt sorry for the poor bloody Burmese. The Japs had played merry hell with every village we came to. Not much standing above ground but weeds and elephant grass, and all the food gone. The natives welcomed us with open arms and we gave them what we could from our air drops. And when an American portable hospital got through, on mules, it was a blessing for them as well as us.

'We finally made it down to Naga Junction in the middle of December, where we met up with 19th Indian Division. They'd got across the Chindwin and had been marching for days to link up with us. We were mighty pleased to see each other, I can tell you.'

While the 36th was pushing down the corridor, General Stilwell had been recalled to the United States, assigned to the training of American land forces. Lieutenant General Dan Sultan had taken command of the NCAC, now comprising five Chinese divisions and the Mars Force, which had absorbed Merrill's Marauders. Two of the Chinese divisions, together with Mars Force and the native Kachin Levies advanced south from Myitkyina aiming directly at Bhamo, to bring the Ledo Road closer to Lashio and the old Burma Road.

To link up with Mars Force, 36th Division now swung left up the branch line to Katha, and the Irrawaddy:

'We got across the river by raft and sampan. Tricky that was – the monsoon had been going for months and the river was in full flood. But we made it, and the Royal Sussex had the honour of being the first to raise the Union Jack on the far shore.'

Earlier, on 28 October 1944, 31 Squadron had moved back to Agartala to resume operations. On the crew of the newly arrived Flying Officer Taylor, was Colin Lynch, crewed as second pilot:

'But on that first day back on ops I was due for one more day of training, on a new Distance and Homing radar and didn't fly on this mission. It was a flight to the Kabaw Valley, and it turned out things were pretty hot over there.

'On the approach, two of the Daks were attacked by Jap fighters. One of them was badly shot up and the pilot, Flying Officer Brian Standridge, was forced to make a crash-landing. He made a good job of that – all his crew were saved, although some of them were injured. Ackers, the navigator, was mounting the VGO when he took a hail of bullets – which knocked the magazine out of his hands! Despite being hit fifteen times, he recovered from his wounds. But Armstrong, the wireless op was not so lucky. He got a single bullet in his stomach – and died a month later. The other Dak, with the crew I should have been with, was shot down. There were no survivors.

'The same day, I'm walking back through the Orderly Room having completed my day's course, when I scare the living daylights out of my mate, Stan Pedley. "Blimey, Colin," he says, "you're dead!"'

That's when I found out that a day in the classroom had saved my life.'

Chapter 18

The Road to Mandalay

By the end of 1944, the advance of General Slim's Fourteenth Army was gathering momentum. On the night of 3 December, 2nd East African Division, in the van of the world's largest single army, moved into Burma and crossed the Chindwin. They marched over the longest Bailey bridge yet built anywhere by the Sappers – all of 1,100 feet – at Kalewa, the very point where Slim had led the British rearguard over the river, two years before. Then the Allies were in retreat – now they were aiming to drive eastward towards the plain above Mandalay, and rout the Japanese invaders.

General Slim and three of his corps commanders were knighted at Imphal in December. His message to his troops was inspiring: 'In this year we have thrashed the Japanese soldier, man for man, and decisively. Next year we shall smash the Japanese army.'

Slim's plans for the 1945 offensive were threatened by events elsewhere. The Germans' winter Ardennes Forest breakout sucked in Allied resources earmarked for Burma. A Japanese advance to Kunming in China resulted in the withdrawal of two Chinese divisions from the north-east of Burma and three American Squadrons, a total of seventy-five C-47s, from the air supply force. But Mountbatten put on pressure to secure more Dakotas, and in January, 267 Squadron flew in from Italy to Imphal, together with two squadrons of the Royal Canadian Air Force. Welcome relief from Japanese fighters was gained when the Allies' October 1944 invasion of the Philippines led to the withdrawal from Burma of all but a skeleton force of the JAAF.

In November 1944, 31 Squadron returned to their old base at Agatarla for frontline operations. On New Year's Day 1945, they moved headquarters fifty miles south, to Comilla, and on 6 February further south again, to Hathazari, ten miles north of Chittagong. Peter Bray explains:

'With a full fuel load and 7,000lbs of freight, the Dak had a maximum operating radius of 250 miles. The armies were moving fast down from the mountains and into the plains, and would soon be approaching the Irrawaddy and Mandalay. To cover them fully all the transport squadrons had to move forward. When we got to Comilla, 62 Squadron was already there, and at Hathazari we found 117 going strong.

'My logbook shows air drops around the turn of 1945 in the Chindwin, Kabaw and Kale valleys – all east of the Manipur mountains. In the first months of the year we were dropping at Mingin, over the Chindwin and well on the way to Mandalay, and landing at Indainggale. Just twenty miles west of Kalewa and the Chindwin, that was one of the first Jap airstrips in Burma to be captured by the Fourteenth Army, made safe by the RAF Regiment, and used by us.'

Colin Lynch, by now a warrant officer, was making similar entries in his logbook:

'I flew eighteen air drop sorties in December '44 and twenty in January '45, all out over and beyond the Chindwin. It was on one of the January sorties that we lost an engine – the first time I'd had that happen in a Dak.'

Even the redoubtable Wasps were showing the effects of continuous operation in the harshest of conditions, leading to occasional main bearing failures:

'The same month, we flew on a leaflet raid to five towns held by the enemy on the Shan Plateau right over on the Siamese border – it was code-named "Nickel". Those towns took some finding – it was a six-hour roundtrip, in the dark all the way out and all the way back.'

Benny Watts was by this time earning flying pay on 31 Squadron:

> 'Twenty-five rupees a month they promised us, for going on the air dispatch teams, but it wasn't always paid. I used to do several days in a row, and often stayed a while at Imphal, if the Dak got grounded and needed repair. I also clocked up a lot of hours in the second pilot's seat. The Canadian crews were more laidback than the Brits. There was one pilot who wanted to play poker with the other three on the crew, so he said, "Here you are Benny, watch the artificial horizon, oil temperature and pressure and give us a call in an hour." '

Over in the Arakan, the Allies' plan was to press on down the Burmese coast, and capture the airfields needed to cover the armies' advance to Rangoon. At the same time, Mountbatten intended to use the port of Akyab as a base for a combined seaborne invasion of the capital, in a hook around the Irrawaddy Delta. The breakout from the line of the Buthidaung-Maungdaw road tunnels began on 10 December. The 15th Corps, comprising two Indian and two West African divisions, advanced from the tunnels down the Mayu Peninsula. East of the Mayu Range the 81st West Africans moved down the Kaladan Valley. They were again supplied entirely from the air – by 194 Squadron, based at Imphal since September 1944.

The squadron was fast becoming trusted by the troops to bring supplies in on time and in all weathers, earning them the nickname 'The Friendly Firm'. Their workload was so intensive that the normal aircrew complement had to be enhanced by ground crew, flying as dispatchers. John Hart was among them:

> 'The supply missions were pretty much non-stop – we did two or three trips a day sometimes, and quite often flew at night. You didn't have much idea where you were dropping – they didn't tell us, see, in case we crashed and were captured.
>   'We weren't trained in... wotsit's name – jungle escape and evasion. That was down to the pilots. But they did shove a parachute at us before we took off. Mind you, we weren't

trained on them either – just told to jump out and pull the ripcord, was what it came to. We were shown how to use the machine guns. I enjoyed that – blasting away at those target drogues took me back to my time in the Lancs. Some of the older Daks had a sort of hole in each window. I asked what they were for and they said the idea was that any troops in the plane could point their rifles through, to defend it from enemy fighters. I believed 'em – but more dangerous for the Daks than the Japs, if you ask me.

'The loads were mostly those big parapacks – weighed well over 100lbs. The squaddies filled them up and we heaved them up the ramps. We had to stow them where the RAF sergeant air drop leader told us to. He had to get the trim right and have them in the right order – the last for dropping going in first and vice versa. Wouldn't want the Gurkhas getting all the beer and the Brits all the rum, would we?

'Up at the DZs the two of us dispatchers and the drop boss – usually the nav – could handle the ordinary packs, but when it got frantic, the wireless ops might come back to help. Sometimes, there were rolls of barbed wire, or bigger affairs – guns and that – with two chutes on top. They needed a bit of hauling, and when it was hot, and the Dak was all over the place, it got a bit torrid. If the pilot had to corkscrew the kite to get away from a Jap fighter – then you hung on for dear life.

'Those sorties lasted anything up to three hours, and by the time you'd finished you'd be soaked through, what with the sweat and standing in the slipstream in the rain. Bloomin' noisy it was with the door open all the time and the engines roaring away – mind you, the racket of those Wasps was music to our ears. All the time I was on those drops we never had any engine failures. Even with all that din, you could hear the Nips' anti-aircraft guns having a go at us. In the storms, you could hear the lightning too. And see it – crackling along the wings and round the props.

'Yes, it was flamin' hard work up in those Daks. But those six months I was on the strength of 194 were all right. I was billeted in their mess – good blokes they were.'

By Christmas Day, 15th Corps had cleared the Japanese from the Mayu Peninsula and was poised to attack the Japanese garrisons on Akyab Island, and take the vital airfield. But the first troops to be ferried across the straits found the Jap base deserted – the enemy had committed all their reserves to the lost cause of defending the Mayu Range, and were now in retreat. The thrust down the coast, with its swampy islands and jungle rivers, now became a combined operation with the Royal Navy and its Commandos and carrier borne fighter-bombers, together with the Royal Indian, Canadian, South African and Burmese Navies. With the West Africans cutting off their line of retreat to the east, and seaborne landings encircling them from the south, the Japanese were trapped. With much bloodshed, the vast majority of that among the enemy, the Allies reached Ramree Island by the end of February and overwhelmed its 1,000-strong garrison – of whom no more than twenty surrendered. The engineers of 15th Corps started airfield development immediately.

In the coastal operation, with sea lines of communication secure, ships delivered ashore 18,000 troops, 14,500 tons of stores, 523 mules and 415 vehicles. The troops advancing rapidly to Mandalay and dispersed over the Burmese plains, by contrast had still to rely entirely on the air. To meet the demand, the transport squadrons were now geared up to airlift and air drop an average of 2,000 tons a day. On some days they peaked at 4,000, and totalled 78,000 for the month of March – a record for the campaign. A fair proportion of these stores were being delivered by the US 10th tactical Air Force C-47s to the 36th British Division, forcing their way south out of Myitkyina, and now bolstered by the 2nd Battalion The Buffs, with rifleman Nobby Knowles in their ranks:

'It was just after Christmas '44 that we were marshalled into this Dakota. It was my first flight ever and I was a bit nervous squatting against the fuselage wall. It didn't help when a rivet popped out above my head as we were taking off and rattled around on the floor. It was very, very bouncy – many of the lads suffered really badly from airsickness, but not me, thank God.

'When we landed, we were amazed at the facilities the Yanks had at Ledo – hangars full of Jeeps, tractors, ammo, aircraft and spares – and rations galore. We didn't think so much of the Americans' effectiveness as fighters but their supply chain was unbelievable. Do you know, a Yankee quartermaster was probably writing off almost as much as our man had to begin with in the whole of the stores at Comilla. The hairy old sods of the battalion had got a proper trading business going. The Yanks couldn't get enough of our Indian rum, puggle pani – "crazy water", they called it. We were entitled to a rum ration if, as the book said, "conditions remained inclement for 48 hours" – in Burma that was practically all the time. The Gurkhas had a permanent rum entitlement. A case of a dozen bottles would buy half a dozen tins of herring in tomato sauce – six to eight would buy a Jeep.

'We fattened ourselves up at Ledo, and then loaded a whole line of Daks with our equipment and flew down to Myitkyina where we joined up with 36th Division. We found it all pretty well beaten up – the town was in ruins, but the Yanks were well on the way to getting things organised at the airbase. We were detailed to load the Dakotas – everything from parapacks of fuel, water, ammo, and clothing – and Jeeps. They could take two of those, or two half-ton trailers – or a Jeep and howitzer, and its gun crew of seven lads, fully armed. When I started, it used to take us forty-five minutes to load a Jeep – we got that down to five.

'We also humped a lot of soft goods, like rice and grain, in heavy triple bags for low-level free drop. Once, they found that four of the Daks were flying tail heavy and couldn't tell why. Then someone had a brainwave. They lifted up the rear floor panels and found masses of rice down there, all swollen up in the damp.

'Then there were the mules. One morning, a Dak came in with dents in the fuselage – from the inside outwards. A big burly sergeant from the RAOC shouts out, "'Ere, you're 2nd Buffs – you're mule men. There's a mule running amok in there, kicking the kite to death. Get in and sort it out." We let

him know in no uncertain terms it was our muleteers that
handled mules, and that he wouldn't get us going in there,
not for a month's extra pay. They had to shoot the poor
beast.'

Meanwhile, the NCAC was pressing south from Myitkyina, and
at the end of December 1944, an American trained Chinese
Expeditionary Force, after seven months' hard fighting at the
cost of 19,000 dead, forced its way across the mountains of
Yunnan and down to Bhamo. By the end of January 1945, the
two forces had linked up, and the Ledo Road had at last reached
the old Burma Road. The land route to Chungking was
complete. The first convoy rolled over the frontier on 28 January.
Stilwell's road had taken 15,000 US soldiers and 35,000 native
labourers three years to drive through some of Asia's densest
jungles.

By the end of the month, the main force of 36th Division had
crossed the Irrawaddy at Katha, and were pressing on their next
objective, the town of Mong Mit, some 100 miles south in the
Shan States, and across the Shweli River. The 2nd Battalion the
Buffs moved down the railway corridor to relieve 10th
Gloucesters. Nobby was in a 'B' Company platoon, assigned as
'Number Two' on a Bren gun section:

'I had to lie prone by the side of the gun and change the
magazines. A little later I was promoted to lance jack and
became "Number One". I found the Bren a mite too accurate
for jungle fighting – you couldn't usually see the Japs, so you
had nothing to aim at. But they were everywhere. It was
unnerving to advance through the lalang – the elephant
grass – where every clump could be hiding one of 'em. The
Bren could have done with a bit more spread.'

The infantry were supported by artillery barrages, but the lads
had to be wary:

'We couldn't trust the gunners to be that accurate, nor the
occasional air to ground support, neither. The Hurribombers
could aim straight, and so could the Beaufighters – the Japs
called them "Whispering Death", they were so quiet coming

in. But the Americans' Thunderbolts were as likely to shoot us up as they were the Japs. The best was to rely on tried and tested fire and movement sweeps.

'We got our air supply mainly from the Yanks, from their Dakotas and Curtiss Commandos, and without all that we just couldn't have survived. It was pretty monotonous food – mostly bully beef, dehydrated vegetables and potato – but food it was. The Japs didn't seem to have any. We saw hundreds of dead ones – mostly they were all swollen with malnutrition, and beri-beri. It was disease that was the big enemy in the campaign. Jaundice, dysentery, scrub typhus and great suppurating jungle sores – we had the lot.

'When we got to the Shweli River, opposite Myitson village, two companies of us went across in sampans. It was too quiet on the river, and when we got up the bank on the far side we found out why. The Japs came at us in swarms, yelling and shooting from the hip. We let loose at them with everything we had – and just held them. But their field of fire commanded the river and our second reinforcing attack got smashed up. We were trapped. We fought it out until nightfall, when our lads came across in sampans, got us survivors out, and dug in. Bloody brave that was – and they held that bridgehead for seven days.

'The 26 Brigade managed to cross the river eight miles further up, get a pontoon bridge over and fight their way down to come up from the rear. Myitson was taken on 9 February, but it took us a few days more to clear the Japs from the area. Then we regrouped, and it was onwards to Mandalay.'

General Slim, now in command of the twenty divisions of Eleventh Army Group, was denied the decisive battle he wanted out on the plains to the north of the Irrawaddy by the Japanese retreat behind the river, where they regrouped in defence of Mandalay. Time was now pressing for the Allies as the monsoon was no more than two months away. They needed to get to Rangoon before it broke and the floods swamped them.

Then at the end of February, Chiang Kai-shek launched an offensive of his own on the Japanese in China, and Slim was told that not only was the Chinese Expeditionary Force to be withdrawn from Burma, but also that the USAAF transport squadrons, then supplying the Chinese and 36th Division, would be required to fly them out. This was at a time when maximum effort was needed from the air supply organisation. It took Mountbatten himself to ease the crisis by persuading the US Chiefs of Staff to allow most of their transports to remain in Burma until the capture of Rangoon, or 1 June, whichever was the sooner. Slim's advance continued, with the squadrons stretched to the limit, and time even more pressing.

The Allies sent in a right hook move to cross the Irrawaddy and attack the main enemy base at Meiktila, 100 miles to the south, from the rear, prior to a pincer assault on Mandalay itself. The Japanese committed their full available force to defend Meiktila and the battle continued for the whole of March, the airfield changing hands many times. From dawn on most days, the RAF Regiment carried out a couple of hours of exposed sweeps to clear the strip of the enemy before the Dakotas could land with vital ammunition, fuel and reinforcements. The final capture of Meiktila, the logistical heart of the Japanese Fifteenth Army, turned out to be the key to the battle of the plains. The enemy's High Command themselves dubbed the bold concealed hook from the south as 'General Slim's master-stroke'.

Allied divisions fought their way across the Irrawaddy to the north, and the assault on Mandalay was unleashed on 19 February. By 7 March the Allies, assisted by overwhelming close air to ground support, were at the gates. After dogged Japanese resistance, the town fell two weeks later.

After the battle, Bill Slim issued the following Order of the Day to the Fourteenth Army:*

'You have won the battle for central Burma. It has been no easy triumph. You have won it against the obstacles of nature, and against numerous, well-equipped and vicious enemy. You have earned victory by the skill, boldness and resolution of corps, divisional and brigade commanders,

* Extract from General Slim's archive courtesy of his son, Viscount Slim.

and by your refusal to let difficulties overcome you, by your grim endurance, unquenchable fighting spirit and magnificent audacity.

'You have advanced for hundreds of miles at unexampled speed over mountains, through jungles and across arid plains, making your own roads, cutting your own tracks, building your own boats, and always against cunning, fanatical opposition. You have forced the heavily defended crossings of two great rivers. These crossings you carried out with meagre equipment, supplemented only by what you could make with your own hands or capture from the enemy. You have driven seven enemy divisions from long prepared positions of his own choosing, which he was ordered to hold to the last. He has fled leaving 18,000 counted corpses on the ground and over 300 guns in your hands.

'Every corps, division and brigade has played its part in this Fourteenth Army victory. None could have done what it did without the help of the others. There could not have been any victory without the constant ungrudging support of the Allied Air Forces. The skill, endurance and gallantry of our comrades in the air, on which we have learnt so confidently to rely, have never failed us. It is their victory as much as ours.

'Every man of the Fourteenth Army and of the Air Forces which flew with it can be proud of his share in this battle. I cannot tell you how proud I am of the men I command. That pride is felt too in your homes, in the Britain, India, Nepal and Africa you have defended, and in the Burma you are liberating.

'We have advanced far towards final victory in Burma, but we have one more stage before it is achieved. We have heard a lot about the Road to Mandalay: now we are on the Road from Mandalay.

'The Japanese are mustering their whole remaining strength in Burma to bar our path. When we meet them

again, let us do to them what we have done before, and this
time even more thoroughly.

8 April 1945
W.J. Slim Lieutenant-General
General Officer Commander-in-Chief'

From January to the end of March, the Allies had advanced 300
miles to take Mandalay. In that time, the transports of Eastern
Air Command had carried more than a million tons of stores
and weapons forward to the battle fronts. It was the supply
aircrews, the ground crews who kept the transports flying and
the men who toiled to load them, who had succeeded so far in
keeping the divisions in business. Now they had to keep them
going the rest of the way – to Rangoon.

Chapter 19

The Race to Rangoon

When Colin Lynch had completed his first tour of 500 operational hours, and started on another, the total maximum hours were reduced from 1,000 to 700. But those whose second tour had started had to complete it. This he did in March 1945, at Hathazari:

'I finished my 1,000 hours in March '45. Even then, I had to apply for a posting. While the letter was being processed I managed another eighteen hours on Flight Lieutenant Dick Riddout's crew. I'd flown a grand total of 326 sorties.

'I'd asked for a posting to my home town, New Delhi, and got it. I found it a bit of a wrench to leave the squadron, and was sad to lose my pals. Of those who joined up with me in '42, Charlie Mann – he was on "A" Flight and I was on "B" – had had a close call at Myitkyina. A Jap bullet grazed his neck. But he survived, and together with me and half a dozen others completed two 1,000-hour operational tours in Burma.

'Others of my boyhood pals did not survive. Clifford Abrahams was killed flying a Hurricane on ops in Burma, as was Desmond Crawshaw, in a Spitfire. I also lost several friends from my home town including Ed Grenier who was killed in a Spit, and Philip Marley. There were a lot of casualties in the fighters. I can see now that coming in that top six at ITW and becoming an observer probably saved my bacon. Mind you, a family friend, Tom Townley, was killed flying a 31 Squadron Dakota.'

Peter Bray completed his tour in Burma in the same month as Colin. Apart from a spell of several weeks in hospital with jaundice, followed by seven days of convalescence on the coast, Peter had been on continuous active service in one of the war's most demanding campaigns for over two years, and had completed 2,000 flying hours. He was awarded the DFC for his achievements. His last flight in the theatre was a mail run to Cawnpore and back in the faithful Dakota.

As Peter flew off back to England, Flight Lieutenant Norman Currell was on his way out to Burma as a replacement Dakota captain on 31 Squadron. By December 1944, he had racked up 1,520 hours in his two years (the maximum tour length) as a flying instructor in Canada. It was time to move on:

> 'The Mosquito looked pretty glamorous so that was my first choice. But I was thirty years old – too old, it seems for fighters. I was destined for Transport Command.
>
> 'I first met the Dakota on my conversion course at the Comox Long Range OTU in Vancouver. It was huge! Ninety-nine feet wingspan and about seventy-five feet long, with two mighty radial engines each of 1,750 horse power. But after a twin-engined conversion course on the Expeditor the step up to the Dak was straightforward and I was solo after a few hours dual. It was really just a matter of getting used to the cockpit layout and characteristics of the big beast.
>
> 'I completed the Long Range Transport Course and after two and a half years in Canada, sailed back to the UK on RMS *Queen Elizabeth*. I was one of those pilots selected to do a four hour lookout each day – mainly for submarines. The *Queen Elizabeth* sailed alone as she was expected to avoid trouble because of her speed. The duty was tedious – I certainly never saw any U-boats – but it earned us an extra meal a day, which was a very good thing.
>
> 'When we got to Liverpool, I took the train to Morecambe. I enjoyed a whirl with the girls in the "Floral Hall" and then it was on to London, and a few days' leave in Romford. Rationing was severe, and the V1 "doodle-bugs" were a nuisance – until the fighter boys learned to bring them down

by flying alongside, getting a wing under one of theirs and upsetting the gyroscopes. But the Nazis then sent us the V2s, which came down from a great height. You didn't hear them until they'd exploded – and only then did you hear the scream they had generated on the descent.

'I reported for the six week Transport Close Support course at Leicester East – sixty-five hours of supply dropping, para-trooping and glider towing, in the Dakota. The work with the gliders was exciting. We practised towing them, and when we got used to that, we saw for ourselves what it was like at the end of a towrope. Very unnerving it was, when they unhitched the cable. They let us go at 1,000 feet, and then there was only one way to go – straight down, as fast as you could to avoid enemy ground fire. It was strange with just the rush of the slipstream and no engines to pull you out of trouble. We were briefed to expect a lot of work with those gliders – they told us 2,000 of them had been parked at Greenham Common, ready for the invasion of the Japanese Empire.

'After that, we drew our tropical gear, including a fold-up camp bed, and hung around waiting for our transit to Far East Command.'

At about the same time, April 1945, out in Burma, 31 Squadron was moving 300 miles south to Ramree Island, where it was joined by 117 Squadron. The airbase had been made operational in record time by the engineers, and the Army Service Corps worked around the clock to build up the stocks needed to support Bill Slim's advancing divisions.

The 36th British Division, with Henry Stock and the Shiny 9th, had fought its way the 100 miles down from Katha to Mandalay:

'After Mandalay was taken, I was rather surprised, and very relieved to find I was due for some leave. I had a couple of weeks in Calcutta, where I was billeted in a museum – the army had requisitioned the upper floor. It was one heck of an anti-climax, after all the action over the border. There wasn't much to do – going to the pictures a couple of times

was the height of any excitement. I didn't go back to Burma
– the battalion was posted to Poona, to train for the invasion
of Malaya, which was codenamed "Operation Zipper".'

The 2nd Battalion the Buffs had been severely beaten up in the
Shweli River and Myitson battles, as Nobby Knowles recalls:

'We'd suffered heavy losses, at least 100 killed and another
100 wounded or sick. We were pulled out. They trucked us
to Millegarum, then it was into a Dakota for Comilla, the
main base of the Fourteenth Army, where we were "hosed
down" – before being flown on to Visapur for Zipper
training. We'd had our time in Burma.'

Ken Brown, recovered from his bout of jaundice, returned in
December to 33rd Corps HQ, by now at Ye-U, near Shwebo,
where he was assigned to 20th Indian Division at Monywa for
the advance on Rangoon:

'We started out at the end of January and pretty soon fetched
up on the banks of the Irrawaddy. I was taken aback to see
how wide it was – about a mile. You could barely see the
other side and it was going to be a real effort to get across.
With more than some trepidation we got into these twelve-
foot outboard motor boats at a place called Myinmu, and set
off. Halfway over, we ran into a lot of Japanese live stuff.
Machine-gun bullets were whizzing over the water and
shells were exploding all around. But we made it. We
beached the boats and clambered ashore.

'We were operating 177B wireless sets, carried on these
ten-hundredweight Dodge trucks. They had a high roof and
a narrow wheelbase – you had to be careful not to turn them
over. In a lull in the fighting, I managed to get sent up on an
errand to Mandalay. It was in a very bad way after weeks of
bombardment. I remember buying a drink from one of the
locals – he made it from sugar cane, crushed through this
contraption like an old fashioned mangle. That was about
the only bright spot.

'From Meiktila, we chased the Japs down through the Pegu
Yomas hills to Tharawaddy. The way we advanced was by

three divisions – advance, main and rear. After an assault the rear leapfrogged the main and took over as advance, and so on. Once, after a warning of a Jap attack, the corporal said, "Better get the Bren gun out, Ken." So I did. Actually it was the first time I'd done it since basic training, but I remembered the drills – check firing mechanism, sights open, load magazine, safety on. We were all pretty jumpy and didn't get much sleep – Johnny Jap used to hang tin cans with stones in on the barbed wire. The rattling was meant to keep us guessing, which it did. But no Japs came – in fact the only ones I saw in the whole advance were dead ones, apart from one very dejected prisoner in a bamboo cage.

'The air supply guys did bloody well by us. They flew those Daks in all weathers to keep us going. Brought us our food, ammo – everything, including free rations of cigarettes. That reminds me, my mum used to send me parcels with four packets of 50 Churchman's Number One – how they got through all the way to the wilds of Burma was a mystery and a wonder to me. I managed once to scrounge a ride in one of the Daks. Indian pilot ran it off the grass – very embarrassed.

'Usually if we did get a bit of free time the only relaxation was to sleep. It was very hot before the monsoon came. We had these canvas water bottles – chagals, they called them. They got damp on the outside and condensation kept the water cool – metal ones used to boil. Toilet arrangements on the advance were basic – a funnel and pipe on a stake in the ground, or a shovel. Once we had a visit from the 20th Indian Div Mobile Bath Unit, with their forty-gallon fuel drums, sawn in half. I took a look, but didn't indulge.

'One day at Magwe, I hitched a ride in an American L-5 light aeroplane. The Yankee pilot seemed very laidback to say the least – at one point he had his foot up on the cockpit coaming and chucked me over a packet of gum. But he couldn't half fly it – landed it on a sixpence.'

At Akyab and Ramree on the coast, engineers rebuilt and re-equipped the harbours, and stocks poured in over the Bay of Bengal. The Dakotas carried them forward to the troops now following the railways and roads alongside the Irrawaddy and Sittang, down the 340 miles from Meiktila to Rangoon. Air supply was now being supplemented by goods carried down the great Burmese rivers on the waterborne flotillas built by soldiers out of local materials.

While the strategic bombers pinpointed the enemy base infra-structure, British, American and Indian fighter-bombers blasted their troops, vehicles and tanks on the frontlines. The air supply crews doubled their flying hours and ground and supply staff worked through the night to achieve their task – but it was still a close run thing. For most of the advance, the Allied soldiers were on half rations – but they never lacked for ammunition.

A highly mechanised formation of 4th Corps drove straight down the Toungoo road, and with tanks and armoured cars in the van, reached the town by the third week of April, as the pre-monsoon winds were at their height, and moved on to Pegu by 1 May. It had advanced 300 miles in a month. The Japanese stragglers on both sides of this bold thrust were mostly mopped up by Karen guerrillas and the Burmese National Army, a force of 7,000 trained soldiers under Aung San, which had adopted the title of 'Patriot Burmese Forces' and transferred its loyalty from the Japanese just in time for the Allied counterattacks.

To the west, the divisions of 15th Corps in the southern Arakan pressed hard on the beaten Japanese, to keep them from joining the enemy's main army in the Burma plain. Around the oilfields of Yennangyaung, 33rd Corps fought a stand-up battle in the 102 degree heat, until a series of armoured hooks broke the enemy line. By 2 May the Allies had occupied Prome, 160 miles from Rangoon.

Meanwhile, a bold 300-mile combined operation had been launched on the Burmese capital from Akyab. Six convoys of 15th Corps troopships, minesweepers and landing craft were routed around the Irrawaddy delta and up the twenty miles of shifting currents, shoals and minefields of the harbour approaches. On 2 May, as the ships approached the capital, a Gurkha paratroop attack cleared the enemy guns at the threatening Elephant Point.

The landing craft, packed with soldiers, motored up the river, soon to be hailed energetically from an oncoming sampan by two RAF officers. Wing Commander Saunders and Flight Lieutenant Stevens reported that on a reconnaissance mission in their Mosquito over Rangoon that morning, they had seen painted on the roof of the jail, two messages from the Allied POWs inside – 'Japs Gone' and 'Exdigitate'. They had landed, and found that the Japanese, their forces cut to pieces out on the plains, had retreated. As a consequence, a brace of British aircrew had been able to liberate Rangoon – and just in time. The very next day, two weeks early, the monsoon arrived.

The columns of 4th Corps came forward from Pegu to occupy the town, while the assault forces of 15th Corps drove the sixty miles up the road to Tharrawaddy, where it linked with 33rd Corps on 17 May. The Rangoon River had been opened to shipping on 6 May, and supply vessels came in two days later. But air supply continued with the same intensity, despite the monsoon, as mopping up operations against the still stubborn Japanese continued throughout southern Burma. A newly con-stituted Allied Twelfth Army fought for three months to advance through the now flooded paddy fields and along the narrow Mawchi road to liberate the port of Moulmein. The aircrews flew on in support – under the 100-feet cloud base and through the teeming rain.

Burma had been liberated, the road to China reopened, and India had been made safe. The campaign objectives handed down to Mountbatten had all but been achieved.

Chapter 20

Victory in Burma

The Dakotas of 267 Squadron RAF had flown in from their exploits in Italy, to arrive at Imphal in February 1945. Derrick Hull was with them:

'I'd hardly had time to settle into my basha, and get used to the jackals howling at night, when I was sent off with a detachment to Maunybin. This was a temporary strip east of Akyab, where the Daks were flying up to three sorties a day and we were pretty busy. By the time the monsoon came, the engineers had managed to get the all weather strip built at Akyab Main, so we moved there, and it got even more hectic.

'The planes were flying all day, so we fitters had to work at night. I was doing up to a dozen DI's in a row – perched fifteen feet up a ladder to get to the instruments in the aircraft's nose. We didn't have any hangars – imagine it, out in the open until four in the morning, in thunder and lightning and pouring rain, and under attack from these huge flying beasties going for the Tilley lamps. And when there was a lull in the weather, the racket from the frogs and cicadas kept us all awake. But we certainly never got bored.

'For a change, I flew on two missions from Akyab, as supernumerary dispatcher. They didn't give us any parachutes, although there were a couple in the wireless operator's position where the pilots stored the survival equipment. I was stood by the open cargo door, heaving the stuff out – rain poured in and I used to get soaked. They'd started to make forward landing grounds on the other side of the Irrawaddy, draining paddy fields and bulldozing the bungs around the edges. That's where we dropped the parapacks. We still had to watch out for the Jap machine guns though – all very exciting.

'But then I flew up to Imphal, and saw one Dakota with the Bailey bridge girders it had been carrying sticking through the fuselage skin – they'd come loose in a cu-nim cloud. Then another one landed, full of bullet-holes. I decided it was just a bit too exciting.

'In any event ground crew volunteers weren't needed by then – the British and Indian Army Service Corps got more of their soldiers and Sepoys onto the loading and dispatching. So they had to do all the sweating and struggling.

'Anyway, one aircraft had bought it in a storm and the bosses didn't want to risk their precious fitters on missions. The monsoon weather made it uncomfortable and dangerous enough on the ground already. The runway was made of metal strips laid on sand – the rain washed the sand away and the bolts of lightning blasted the metal, turning the runway into a switchback. There was a fair number of crashes.

'We airmen were billeted in tents – small they were, four beds maximum. You could hardly stand up straight in them. Ours were in a grove of palm trees and in any sort of wind you were in mortal danger from a coconut attack. Our charpoys were pretty basic bamboo affairs but I'd managed to scrounge a folding bed from Italy, so I was all right. Anyway, we were better off than some. "A" and "B" flights' ground crew had to put up with old fuel tanks, cut in half long ways, for their flight offices but our Instrument Section workshop was in an EPI tent, the sort used for stores. If you got those as a billet, they were tall enough to stand up in and could take a dozen beds.

'It rained for three months solid – kit was always mouldy, there was mud everywhere and we were never dry. There was a shower made out of a forty gallon drum drilled with holes, but it was quicker to strip off and wash down in the rain.

'I specialised in autopilot repairs. One of the Flight

Commanders, a squadron leader, didn't know how to work what he called "this new-fangled thing". So of course the lads got pretty fed up with him bouncing the kite around the sky. So they sent me up with him to show him what was what. His crew bought me a few beers for that.'

In May, Benny Watts was sent from Ramree on a 31 Squadron detachment to Toungoo, over on the banks of the Sittang:

'The Fourteenth Army was advancing so fast that to keep up, the transport squadrons had to move to these forward bases, right up near the front. The Japs were still all around so we were glad to see the RAF Regiment there with their armoured cars. From Toungoo we were flying missions over Siam, making drops to Allied strongpoints, and the hush-hush units – native guerrilla fighters led by British SOE officers, who'd been landed behind the lines in Lysanders. They were looking for Allied POWs reported to be wandering in the hills, escaping from the camps.

'It was hard going on those sorties – the pre-monsoon winds gave us merry hell, and the drops were a long way from base, right up-country. I remember on one trip seeing a herd of elephants, wallowing in a lake. After one particularly dicey trip, our Canadian pilot celebrated our successful return by beating up the airfield. He really wanted to do a run in and break, but that was pretty unimpressive in a Dak. So he flew in low between two trees – and the prop-wash blew the cookhouse tent down.'

In March, 62 and 194 Squadrons had moved forward to Maunybin, the 'Friendly Firm' having added a casualty evacuation flight to its strength, operating L-5 Sentinels. Up at Hathazari remained 117, covering the northern areas, until in May it too moved south, to join 31 at Ramree.

From 1 June, following the liberation of Rangoon, all units of the USAAF moved out of Burma, their job well done, to join the American forces in China and the Pacific. The RAF Dakotas took on all supply dropping and trooping missions, and continued operating the China air bridge flights for two more months. To these tasks was added the air rescue of thousands of Allied POWs. The push was on to mount an invasion of Siam, Malaya and Singapore, to free those known to be held starving and suffering in the camps there.

Norman Currell had been given a few days leave before he was to report to Swindon for the flight to Karachi. As luck would have it, the last night of that leave, 8 May, coincided with VE Day celebrations:

> 'I went up to London and joined the high-spirited crowd who were making the most of the fact that the war in Europe was over at last. And here was I getting ready to play my part in the war against Japan!
>
> 'The next day our crew gathered in Swindon. We had a second pilot, navigator, wireless op and our newly acquired engineer, for the glider snatch ops. We took off in a brand new Dakota for Karachi – across France to Sardinia, then Alexandria and Sharja, and across Iran to India – forty-five hours in the air.
>
> 'We had been flying at about 8,000 feet at quite a pleasant temperature, but as we descended to 6,000 we could feel the heat. And on the ground it was really hot – and the smell! We were in Karachi for fourteen days where we had the usual dose of the "squitters" and fought to keep the "shite-hawks" away from our food. We got used to the smell of camel dung, and of the beggars, but not of the dead bodies lying in the streets. We didn't know what poverty was until we saw it in Karachi in '45.
>
> 'We flew on from Karachi in a Sunderland. That made us chuckle – we'd flown all the way over the ocean in a Dakota and now all the way over the sub-continent in a flying-boat. We had four days in Calcutta and then set off by bus, ferry and "Shanks's pony". We lugged our gear through the glorious scenery of the Ganges Delta to Comilla – that was the HQ of Far Eastern Command then.
>
> 'The next day, an RCAF Dakota flew in to take us down to 31 Squadron's base at Ramree Island. We staged through Meiktila where we saw the burnt-out tanks, and all the other

debris from the Fourteenth Army's advance and the Japs' retreat.

'We arrived at Ramree on 20 June. It was in the middle of the monsoon season. Anywhere else, flying would have been scrubbed because of weather but we flew through it to deliver supplies to the army on the far side of the Irrawaddy. We had a couple of familiarisation flights with the Canadian crew and then we were off on our own. We took the loads to places with, to us, strange names like Toungoo, Myingyan, Mingaladon and Meiktila. We'd do three trips every other day or so. The first trip each morning would be in very heavy rain, until we got over the coastal mountains and then it'd be clear sailing until the Irrawaddy.

'On the second trip, cumulous clouds would be building up and by the time we were making our third trip they'd be a real headache. They'd tower way over 20,000 feet, far too high for us to think about going over them. So we had to go through them – lightning flashes and violent turbulence all the time. It was nothing to find the Dak dropping 1,000 feet or more, then a few seconds later lifting back up again. Of course, all this was done in a heavy layer of cloud so there was no chance of actually seeing the thunderhead. But we found that if the radio compass was set just right, it would pick up the disturbance from the lightning and point directly at it. So we could veer thirty degrees off our heading and work our way around the worst of the trouble.

'There was no radio beacon yet at the base, so the only thing to do on return, was to fly out well past the coast and the airfield, let down over the ocean till we got below the cloud and then work our way back. Somehow we made it, every time. We counted ourselves lucky – during June and July, eighteen of the Ramree Dakotas were lost to the weather.

'They'd built the runway with a two-feet layer of sand and on top of this laid a series of steel planks. But the big problem was that the sand was undermined by the drenching rain and the weight of a Dakota would bend the planking. Then the ends would stick up in the air. Of course, we'd have to circle in the murk while the ground engineers made running repairs.

'We made isolated supply drops to small detachments operating in the jungles between the Irrawaddy and the mountains to the east. There was one which particularly sticks in the mind, a place codenamed 'Stornoway', an army strongpoint fifty miles south of Ramree and at about 3,000 feet. We took off quite early, hoping to get the drop done before the build up of cloud. We found the DZ among the trees but it was so small that we had only a short time for each run, which meant we had to make many more runs than we'd hoped for. Cloud kept drifting in, so we were all the time heading out to sea until we found a reasonably large break – and then following the clear spot to Stornoway. We had to fly out directly into the wind and then back with it right behind us to give as a chance of being over the DZ – there wasn't time to search for it.

'The drop took a good two hours longer than we or the Ops Officer had planned – there was considerable speculation that we had come to grief. When we eventually made it back, we were pretty whacked. But the next day the Intelligence Officer showed us a signal from the soldiers down there, saying thank you for the supplies and for our persistence in getting the delivery made. Needless to say, we were chuffed that our efforts had been acknowledged.

'We carried on ferrying supplies until early August. Then I was called to the Squadron Commander's office and told I was nominated to take charge of a small advance party detailed for special training for an impending operation. This turned out to be leading the planned attack on Singapore and Bangkok with gliders and paratroops. But it never got to happen.

'The very next morning the news came through that the Americans had dropped "two big bombs" and the Japanese were suing for peace.'

By this time, Ken Brown had been two months at Tharawaddy, billeted in a Burmese house:

'In July, I'd met four wonderful girls from the Women's Auxiliary Services Burma – "WAS(B)s". They were the valiant ladies who manned these mobile canteens right up on the frontline, all through the campaign. One night this quartet stopped their Jeep outside our basha and asked if we had anything to drink. We had a crate of Aussie beer, the sergeant found a bottle of scotch and we had a pretty good party. On the whole, I was quite enjoying myself – so it was with mixed feelings that I got the news that my number had come up on the leave rota.

"Where would you like to go?" says the sergeant. "Brighton," says I.

'What I did, was to sail on the *Devonshire* to Calcutta and then go on the Himalayan Railway to the pine trees, clubs and pony rides of Darjeeling. On the way back, in Calcutta, a mate stops me.

"Have you heard the news Ken? They've dropped a bloody big bomb on a place called Hiroshima."

'Then we heard there'd been a second one, on Nagasaki – and the Japs had surrendered.

'When I get back to Tharawaddy the Company Sergeant Major says, "Don't bother to unpack Brown – you're off to Bangkok in the morning."'

Throughout the dramas in the south of Burma, Richard Hull was over on the borders of Afghanistan – in Quetta on his Group 1 training:

'The camp was at 5,500 feet and it was brass monkeys cold – umpteen below zero and deep snow. It was a real shock to the system. To get there we'd travelled through Calcutta where it was ninety-four in the shade! Mind you, it had been pretty chilly in Imphal in January – but nothing like that. A couple of poor bloody Gurkhas froze to death on guard duty. Then the bridge approaching the camp collapsed and we were cut off. Anything made of wood was burnt for fuel. We were there for Christmas '44. Awful that course was, and it lasted six long months – until VE-Day.

'Things didn't get much better when they sent us on jungle training. That was at Belgaum, south of Poona. It was in a

bubonic plague area and the camp was swarming with rats
– they kept on eating the bloomin' soap!

But I had a bit of luck when there were hold ups in the
training and I got posted to the radio maintenance section of
267 Squadron – where I met up with my brother!'

Brother Derrick takes up the story:

'After the Japanese surrender, 267 moved to Mingaladon
airfield, outside Rangoon. We were billeted in the old
barracks – weather and war beaten, but not too bad. When
the monsoon cleared, the weather became much more
pleasant and we managed some trips downtown. I visited
the Shwe-Dagon Pagoda and saw gangs of Jap prisoners
working on the pipeline – served them bloody well right.

'Our Daks were flying in more and more released Allied
POWs. Poor beggars – they were so emaciated that forty or
fifty of them could be carried in one go, in an aircraft
designed to take just two dozen troops, maximum.'

Richard remembers a particularly harrowing incident:

'One of the planes took off one morning to take a bunch of
released prisoners and time expired men up to Calcutta.
Happy as sand boys they were – waving and cheering. The
Dak crashed en route – none of the crew and passengers
survived.'

When the Burma Campaign had been won, Field Marshal Lord
Wavell, who was installed as Viceroy in India at the end of the
war, wrote:

'I have soldiered for more than forty-two years, and the
more I have seen of war the more I realise how it all depends
on administration and transportation (what our American
Allies call logistics).'

There had never before been a logistical requirement quite like
that in south-east Asia. Each day, the Fourteenth Army alone
needed 2,000 tons of rations and that in an area of mountain,
jungle, swamp and dust 1,000 miles long.

It wasn't all about supply by air. The Assam-Bengal railway was rebuilt to carry 3,000 tons a day to Manipur and as much again to Ledo. Roads had to be built – in 1942 the force of labourers from the Indian Tea Association that built the road in the Chin and Manipur hills grew to 82,000 at its peak. On those roads, Sepoy drivers delivered 3,000 tons of all kinds of freight every day to the advancing soldiers, over a land supply route which, in the end, stretched 400 miles through the jungle. Thousands of long-suffering mules, horses, donkeys, oxen and elephants humped their loads over punishing terrain. Later in the campaign, on the rivers, craft of all types – many of them built by the soldiers themselves out of logs and creepers – were pressed into service as a supply line.

But the Allies' plans for the 1944-45 counterattack in Burma were built around an aerial delivery system. Air Supply and Air Transportation staffs were set up, to work closely with Troop Carrier Command. Supply bases with logistics outfits were established at key points, and from the Battle of the Admin Box in February 1944, when 3,000 tons were flown in, they were working at full tilt until the end of the campaign – and for some time after.

During the sieges of Imphal and Kohima, in 8,000 sorties, two and a half army divisions were flown in by air, and 76,000 tons of supplies delivered. The load manifests tell their own story: 400 tons of sugar and 1,300 of grain, 850,000 gallons of petrol and 7,000 of rum, 27,000 eggs for the hospitals, 43 million cigarettes – and 12,000 bags of mail from home.

Chapter 21

First In, First Out

The Far East war was over for most of our veterans, but not by any means for all. Some had already gone home. In May 1944, after weeks of touring Vera Lynn had begun to suffer from prickly heat:

'I was flown out to the hillstation at Shillong to recuperate and it was up there that I met Lady Slim. All through the trip I'd had no letters from home and got very little in the way of news. It wasn't until I was well on the way back that I heard about D-Day. I flew in a Dakota to Bombay, and then it was a Sunderland again – sitting on those excruciating metal seats all the way to England. And when we finally got there, we had the doodlebugs.'

In September the same year, on his twenty-first birthday, George Hufflett embarked on the New Zealand hospital ship *Rangitata*, bound for England:

'That ship was a much better affair than the one I'd gone out on – you could even open the portholes for some light and air. But when we got to Port Taufiq at the bottom end of the Suez Canal, my arm – still in plaster – was not very good at all so off I went to another hospital. It took a while to fix me up and I had to get on a train to Port Said, where all they could come up with was this old troopship, the *Stratheden*. It didn't half wallow around in the Med but there weren't any U-boats or anything like that. We picked up a convoy, the first to go through the Irish Sea. It was non-stop to Liverpool.

'I had a week in the staging camp at Southport and then

was sent south by train. I arrived in Lewes in the middle of
the night and had to wake up my elder sister May, to beg a
bed. I got on the bus the next morning and was back with
Mum and Dad, for Christmas. You won't believe this, but the
pay book I lost on Jail Hill was there on the sideboard,
posted home from Burma. It all seemed like a dream
somehow, all that time out there – unreal. I felt really strange
for a long time.

   'They took the plaster off my arm at St Mary's Hospital in
Eastbourne. The skin graft wasn't doing well at all, so they
packed me off to Guy's Hospital in Orpington. There I had
what was called a pinch graft and then it was back into
plaster again. I remember going with a whole bunch of other
patients, all of us bandaged up, to a Chelsea football match.
The fans took one look at us and gave us a wide berth, thank
goodness. Anyway, finally they take the plaster off, and I'm
sent for physiotherapy in Eastbourne, three times a week.
What a palaver it all was. In the end I got my discharge from
the army on St George's Day 1945.'

It was five weeks before that date that Peter Bray left Agatarla
for England with a posting to long-range transports. He
embarked on a Solent flying boat and was re-united with Phyllis
on 1 April. In May, after a three-week conversion course in
Yorkshire, he began a series of trooping flights in the Liberator.
He was back in Karachi in June and was in Calcutta when the
Japanese capitulated in August. He served on Transport
Command until May 1946 and his last flight before demobilisation was out of Waterbeach.

Out in the Far East after the Japanese surrender, there was
trouble brewing among the British forces. The war in Europe
had ended three months before, and demobilised men were
already flooding onto the job market at home. The war in the
east was supposedly also over but the first-in, first-out system
meant that thousands of conscripted soldiers, sailors and
airmen had to wait for repatriation until their number came up.
There were further delays, before a berth or aircraft seat became
available. There was a fair amount of strife from those who
thought they should come first in the queue.

Derrick Hull was one of the luckier ones. In December 1945, after four years on active service, he became time expired, and grabbed a flight to Calcutta in a 267 Squadron Dakota:

'Then, after a five-day stay at Dalbungarh, a mate and I were allocated a lift in a Canadian Liberator bound for England. We had to sit with twenty army lads on bum-breaking wooden seats fixed up in the bomb bay. It took a while to get out of India as the crew flew first to Delhi and then down to Karachi, to fill every spare space with carpets and rugs. Eventually we reached Palestine, where we had to wait for three days. It was wet and cold and they wouldn't let us visit Tel Aviv – British servicemen were already being attacked down there. We spent another four days at Castel Benito, in North Africa, where it was boiling hot. It was cooler over the Alps – bloody freezing to be frank – and we were more than happy to see the English coast. We raised a cheer when the pilot did a fifty-feet low pass over the white cliffs of Dover. But when we landed at RAF Oakington in Cambridge, these poker faced, pinstriped Customs blokes rifled through all our cases. Welcome home, heroes!

'We managed to grab some tea in the mess, before jumping on the night train south. By two in the morning next day, I was shivering in a Southampton phone box, speaking to Vera, who was in the WAAFs at Spitalgate. We were both home by Christmas.'

In Burma, petty crime in the Forces was widespread and the odd mutiny boiled up. Nobby Knowles has a few thoughts about that:

'In the battles, the vast majority of conscripts seemed to accept their fate, and pitched in with the best of them. Skivers were in the minority and the army handed them on the spot punishments or, for persistent offenders, penal servitude of up to three years. But after VJ-Day there was a lot of trouble. There were these cartoons with "Chad" saying, "Wot No LIAP?" LIAP stood for "Leave In Anticipation of Posting", which gave you a troopship passage and then twenty-eight days' leave in Blighty.'

As the lads started to leave in some numbers, those remaining had their work cut out getting the work done, and in the anti-climax of peace, keeping their spirits up.

The Army Service Corps took over as dispatchers on the Dakotas of 194 Squadron and John Hart found himself posted back to New Delhi:

'There wasn't much going on there. At Christmas, to cheer us up, they gave us all two bottles of Indian beer. Then there were ENSA shows and once, a team of UK professional foot-ballers came out. They were all RAF sergeants, Physical Training Instructors. I remember there was a Welsh interna-tional goalkeeper, Roy John, an England batsman and Arsenal winger, Denis Compton, and also George Robinson, a heavyweight boxing champion from Leeds. I got a bit of leave and for a change of scene, went down to have a look at Batavia in Java. It wasn't much of a holiday there though – the Indonesian Nationalists were giving us Europeans a lot of stick.

'At last, early in '46, I got shipped home to Liverpool. My final memory of the sub-continent was the mobs in Delhi shouting, "Jia Hind!" – Quit India! Thank you very much, I thought, I will. When I got back to the old base in Blackpool to be demobbed, it was after work on a Friday. The civvies wouldn't work on a Saturday so I had to wait until the Monday to get signed off. Welcome back to Blighty.'

Also in New Delhi, was Colin Lynch, living in the family home at Connaught Place and having a busier and better time than John. He rode his bike to his job in the Air Booking Centre:

'Occasionally – although I didn't have a driving licence – I'd drive the old family Ford Tourer. I was one of the three shift leaders, handling flights for the airlines, Tata amongst them, as well as for the RAF. With so many going back to Blighty we were never short of work.

'It was good living at home. The Ford got a lot of use for hunting and shooting trips, and picnics. And Delhi, with its cinemas, night clubs, shopping and girls, provided a pretty good social life. Then my name came up for demob in August 1946. They gave me the option of being demobbed either in India or in England. I thought for a bit about staying out there but reckoned that the political, racial and religious disharmony pointed to tragic times ahead. I chose England. I left on the SS *Canton*, first-class, with my own cabin.'

The ship sailed through the Suez Canal and the Med. Colin set foot in England, for the first time in his life, in Southampton, where he took the train to Kirkham outside Blackpool. There, a good time was to be had with the girls, before he was demobbed.

In Rangoon, Richard Hull served on 267 Squadron until the end of June 1946:

'I did manage a month's leave in England in the spring – sailed on the P&O steamship *Ormond* – and was just in time for my brother's wedding. Back in India, I took a boat from Calcutta to Rangoon – and found 267 disbanding. There was just one kite left, and we last blokes loaded it up with all our kit and took off for Singapore. Bad weather forced us to land at Butterworth, where we tried for an outing to Penang Island. But over there they had a smallpox epidemic – so we took off again, risking the bad weather, to try for Singapore.

'The crew got lost in the pouring rain, before spotting a railway line going in what they thought was the right direction. But we ran short of fuel and had to crash-land. The pilot found what looked like a decent open space but too late, realised it had been sabotaged by the Japs with lengths of railway line stuck up on end. Half of one wing got taken off but we all climbed out of the wreckage alive.

'Before long, a shooting-brake drove up. It was the planter – a Frenchman he was, and he owned the clearing. He'd heard us come down and came to find us. He told us we were near Labis and took us all off to his house for a good meal, a night's sleep and an excellent breakfast.

'The next day the Air Force turned up with trucks to take

us down to Singapore. Later, a salvaging team bolted
another wing onto the Dak and then they could fly it out,
down to Changi. That was our base. We had a wonderful
time there, until they sent us – don't ask me why – on a
jungle survival course. All I got out of that was jungle sores.
I was in hospital with those until I sailed home on the *Queen
of Bermuda*. She was a somewhat elderly Furness Withy ship,
so we didn't quite make it back to Liverpool in time for
Christmas.'

Ken Brown didn't get home until 1947:

'At the beginning of September '45 we took off in a Dak for
Saigon, the first of three planeloads of Major General
Gracie's Control Commission, set up to do the French government's work until they could get back to Indo-China. We
had a company of Gurkhas on board.

'The first day we got as far as Bangkok. We came down the
steps to find ranks of Japs with fixed bayonets, apparently
barring our way. We were a bit taken aback until we realised
it was a Guard of Honour. We were billeted overnight in an
ex-POW camp – eerie that was. There were just plain
wooden huts with narrow bed-boards down each side to
sleep on, and a dirt trench down the middle. We stretched
out on our bed-rolls and tried not to think of what it must
have been like for the prisoners a few months earlier.

'In Saigon the next day we got a right royal welcome from
the locals. The girls were lovely and warm at first, but cooled
off a bit when they realised we were just penniless Anglais
and not rich Americans. But we weren't poor for long. We
got paid in local piastres at four times the rate of our normal
army pay – and were put up in the luxury of the Continental
Palace Hotel, with great French grub. Everywhere we went
we travelled in the British and American vehicles that had
been captured by the Japs – and had Japs to drive us.

'We soon discovered that the Annamite and Vietminh
nationalists had it in for the French, and they didn't think
much of us Brits either – collaborators we were, to them. The
airfield was four miles out of town at Tan Son Nhut and

when it got attacked they brought in the RAF Regiment to deal with it. But we had only that one company of Gurkhas to look after us so it was decided to re-arm the Japs for guard duties. That seemed pretty weird after all the nastiness in Burma but there were 45,000 of them to choose from, still there in Indo-China – and with a bit of prodding they did a pretty good job.

'We felt somewhat isolated over there and it was all very tense, but we had a great time in downtown Saigon – eating a lot of good food and drinking a lot of anisette I met this French Eurasian girl who ran a bar. She wanted to get hold of some weaponry to defend herself and said she'd sleep with me if I'd get her a Sten gun. I had to decline – court-martial offence, and all that.

'It couldn't last for ever and, in January '46, after six months, the French got their act together and we were flown back to India. I was sent to a Signals unit in Calcutta where there were big social changes going on. I was now finding myself stepping off pavements to let Indians pass. It was getting tense there, too – mobs in the streets and all that. One day the tyres of my Dodge truck got set on fire. I was much relieved to get a posting in January '47 to the Doelali Trooping Depot. I was due for transit to dear old England – back to Brighton at last.'

Chapter 22

Conflict Continues

While the others, one by one, were going home, in August 1945 Norman Currell, Nobby Knowles and Benny Watts were re-mustering for training for Operation Zipper. Nobby was flown west to the Indus Delta:

'They sent us over there for the mudbanks. We came in on "Landing Ships Infantry" – LSIs – went down the nets like monkeys and wallowed in the ooze. Then we struggled ashore as best we could. It was hard enough with a rifle and pack – how we would have survived with Brens, ammo boxes and all our other kit, and under fire, is anyone's guess.

'But we were most at risk when we got called out for what they called "Duties in aid of the Civil Powers". The Indian Congress Party were claiming independence and there were riots and all sorts of mayhem going on. The drill was that we'd be trucked out to a disturbance in full combat kit and under the command of the Orderly Officer, form up in two ranks across the road, front on to the mob. We'd stand there all calm and controlled like, with our tin hats on our heads, rifles at the order, while the rioters chanted their "Jia Hind! – Quit India!" Whereupon there'd be a muttering in the ranks, "Wish to Christ we could!"

'The Orderly Officer would by now have sent for a magistrate – while the demonstrators continued to work themselves up into a right old frenzy. Now and again, one of us would take a brick in the chops and be taken off for treatment round the back of the truck – in return, we'd hammer a rifle butt or two onto the bare toes of the nearest rioters. Eventually, the magistrate would arrive. The Officer would order the bloke with the bugle to blow a warning and then he'd read the Riot Act, finishing up with, "Under Order D90A I am empowered to open fire!"

'Next, two of us unfurled a banner reading, in English and in Urdu, "Disperse or We Shall Open Fire". That worked up the crowd even more – but the ringleaders started to shuffle out of harm's way to the rear. Then the officer shouted, "Picket will fix bayonets!" With a fair old clatter, on go the eighteen-inch sword bayonets. Then it's, "Front rank kneel!" and, "Picket, five rounds load!" In go the bullets and you can hear the charger guards rattling onto the ground. Then it's "Picket – take aim. Shoot low to maim!"

'By this time, our show of disciplined force had the first line of demonstrators losing their fervour somewhat and nine times out of ten, the mob dispersed. If they didn't, there was a nominated marksman detailed to take out the chief troublemaker and it was "Picket, fire!" There's a short, sharp volley – and the "Shoot low to maim" order somehow gets forgotten. The mob disperses now, all right.

'Of course, next day there'd be banner headlines screaming about the brutal British imperialist forces. Quite right – but they were brutal times.

'We then went back to the east, and embarked on two light aircraft carriers with the 5th Indian Division. They had a divisional sign with a red ball on a black background, so of course they got called the "Flaming Arseholes", didn't they? We sailed from the Hooghly River at the beginning of September. Off the west coast of Malaya, somewhere between Port Swettenham and Port Dixon, we transferred to the LSIs, and climbed down the nets on to landing craft for the assault. But there was a maze of sandbanks and the helmsmen had to beach the boats about a quarter of a mile out. Down the ramps we went – straight into three or four feet of water, and mud.

'What a shambles! We had to dump a lot of our kit just to keep going – I did manage to keep hold of my rifle. We straggled onto the shore – and looked up to see lines of Japs

waiting for us. Quite a shock, I can tell you. It was a great
relief when we discovered they were there to surrender. We
hadn't been sure – the treaty had only been agreed the
previous week and the news was taking its time getting
around the enemy ranks.'

One hundred thousand men had gone ashore at Port
Swettenham on 9 September. The Japanese surrender at
Singapore was not formally signed by General Itagaki until
three days later, so Nobby and his mates had every reason to be
nervous:

'Progress down the Malay Peninsula was slow. There were
dozens of Jap prison camps with thousands of Allied
prisoners all waiting to be liberated – poor devils. We had to
get them fed and patched up, and then flown out on the
Daks. The Jap guards were still there as well, all of a sudden
wanting to be as nice as pie, the bastards – we had to get
them locked up. Most of them turned out to be North
Koreans – they're taller than your average Jap.

'We had to deal with a fair bit of bolshieness among our
own troops. Some of the Paras were real trouble. They'd
taken a terrible beating in Normandy and at Arnhem and
what was left of them had been reformed and sent straight
out to the Far East. But we got down to Singapore all right.
The only grenades I set off were the ones I used at Endor –
for fishing.'

Follow-up divisions for Zipper were transported to Penang and
Singapore by sea as there were fewer air transports available
now. Number 238 Squadron RAF, which had seen valiant
service with Spitfires in the European Theatre, had been
reformed with Dakotas and arrived in India for supply
dropping and casevac operations in February 1945. But they
moved on to Australia in June. At the end of the year, 117
Squadron was disbanded at Ramree, and two months later, 194
at Mingaladon. It was not to be long before 267 Squadron too
was wound up, in July 1946. Meanwhile, 62 and 31 Squadrons
flew on. The Canadian crews of 31 were called back to Delhi

soon after the Japanese surrender, for transit back to Canada, but for the RAF air and ground crews there was more dangerous work to come.

Norman Currell was detailed to take charge of an advance party at Mingaladon outside Rangoon, and await the arrival of the rest of the squadron from Ramree, en route to Singapore:

'I'd been told to get hold of beer and spirits, so that we could have a victory celebration when the others arrived, so after we'd managed to get some tents put up, we set about getting enough booze for about 300 happy souls. The stuff arrived by the crateful. But then, as usual, it was all changed. The squadron was going to fly direct to Singapore after all. Bit by bit my detachment was sent back to Ramree – and I was left with all that hooch, not yet paid for.

'Well, I let the Messing Officer know that I had all these empty tents – and a bar looking for customers. Before long we had crowds of thirsty RAF blokes lining up, ready to pay top dollar for a drink – and paying off our debt. Everyone was happy!'

Norman rejoined the squadron at Ramree and in September everyone flew off down to Singapore, except for Benny Watts who stayed behind with the clearing up detail. In due course, they set off in an old tub of a ship, towing a barge with all the squadron kit.

Arrived in Singapore, Norman was as busy as ever:

'One of my first flights was to take the Chief of Police and a dozen Chinese big-wigs back to Kuching, 400 miles to the east and the capital of Sarawak in British Borneo. We had several news hounds with us, all looking for stories in the Far Eastern theatre now that Europe was no longer providing such drama as before.

'This was the first Allied flight into Kuching. They'd set up a welcome committee for the VIPs and we were invited to join them. It was in true Chinese style, a grand occasion. Unbeknown to me the navigator and the wireless ops readily made themselves available for comment and a few days later a copy of the *Daily Sketch* was making its way around the mess, with the headline, "Invader Currell They Call Him". They gave me hell in the crewroon for that!

'The facilities at the Changi base were pretty good – the Japs had kept everything in good repair – but we took every opportunity to go downtown. We went there for the food and beer, of course, but also for the two dance halls, the "Happy Hour" and the "Happy World". At each of these places you bought a book of tickets for one Malay Straits dollar and exchanged them for dances with the young women. Then you could make your mind up about any further activity when the dance hall closed at midnight. You could go with a girl to a sort of dormitory down the road that had a series of cubicles, each with a bed, chair and wash-bowl stand. That place was a bit of a passion killer really, so I preferred to go to a girl's private place. Down in her shower room one thing would lead to another – and I'd walk out an hour or two later feeling two feet off the ground.

'The good-time girls across in Java were a different thing altogether. On one trip we brought back more than a full load of about thirty young women – Koreans who had been forced to serve as sex-slaves for the Japs. They carried pathetically few belongings and looked completely worn out and pitiful. We took them up to Penang – where after rest and recuperation they were most likely doomed to a fate pretty much the same as the one they'd just escaped.

'We flew a lot to the Netherlands East Indies. There were hundreds of thousands of Allied POWs to extricate from the Jap prison camps all over south-east Asia, including Java and Sumatra. Over there, thousands of Dutch refugees and ex-POWs were needing help too. Indonesian nationalists had seized power after the Jap surrender and straight away their leader, Sukarno, had proclaimed a republic. So roving bands of them were after the Dutch colonialists, armed to the teeth and looking for blood.

'This all had to be sorted out by the Brits, because the Americans' General MacArthur had handed responsibility for south-east Asia back to Mountbatten. So, on 15

September, the Royal Navy sailed in with three Indian divisions and one of Highlanders, and accepted the Jap surrender. It turned out we'd been pitched into a battle royal once again.'

Nobby Knowles was on one of the troopships, and Benny Watts was soon to join him and the other 90,000 Allied serving men who found their war extended as occupiers of another east Asian country. A detachment of 31 Squadron was sent to Batavia (later Djakarta), on the island of Java and by October, as the situation worsened, the whole outfit relocated there. Benny Watts again had to load up the barge and make another uncomfortable sea passage in an LSI:

'Things were not easy in Batavia – the natives were in no mood to accept us Brits and our Indian allies. They were determined to make our lives as difficult as possible. Of course, it was the Dutch they hated most. We even had to paint out the red centre of the RAF roundels on our aircraft – the red, white and blue looked too Dutch.

'The airfield was at Kemajoran, forty miles along the coast from the town. We were virtually marooned on what was a pretty crummy base, but at least we had the RAF Regiment defending it. There was just the one 1,600-yard runway, made of bithess – a disaster in the rain. And what rain! There were over 100 Allied aircraft operating from the strip – all types, Thunderbolts, Spitfires, Mosquitoes, Austers, Dutch Liberators and Catalinas, and our Dakotas. The runway was swamped, and the rest of the place a sea of mud. Our blokes were flying about thirty sorties a day. It was mayhem.

'But the worst for me was all those ex-POWs. The Indos mixed up who was British and who was Dutch – probably not always accidentally, because we were all colonialists to them – and our troops had to fight to get the poor blighters out of the camps, over to the nearest airstrip, and into our Daks.'

Nobby Knowles was among those troops:

'The 5th Indian Division was sent down to Soerabaya. Some

Dutch prisoners had been told to wait for the relieving troops, but decided to leave camp of their own accord. On 8 October, they defiantly ran up their national flag in the town – and were slaughtered by the mob. It took us a month to sort that lot out. We got the rest of the internees out – 10,000 of them there were – but we took 400 casualties doing it. Things got so bad on the islands that we had to re-arm the effin' Nips and use them to help restore law and order. All the same, the Allies lost well over 2,000 men in the first two months. And back home they all thought the war was over.'

Norman Currell flew over to the new base at the beginning of November:

'We were billeted in a dreadful joint halfway between the city and the airfield. Of course, we wanted to check out the action downtown so I borrowed the Flight Commander's Jeep and we all piled in. We found a bunch of Dutch women who laid on a party in one of the big Batavia hotels. Given the shortage of Dutch men, they were all up for it so, when the curfew came on at nine o'clock and the party was still in full swing, we decided to stay all night.

'Unfortunately, the next morning we found that the Jeep had been disabled by the Indos. We were in deep trouble. I decided I'd walk to the British Embassy to call for help. But I hadn't gone far when I saw a group of maybe ten or twelve locals blocking the road ahead of me. They were loaded down with machetes and knives and I thought, 'Here's where I'm found dead in a ditch'.

'I quickly ran through my options – use my revolver, run or face it out. I decided to keep on walking. When I got up to the Indos, I raised an arm in a gesture of peace and said, as firmly as I could, 'Good morning! I am a British officer'. To my amazement, they let me through without a word. I was still alive.'

The risks on the ground were compounded by those in the air:

'At the beginning of December a couple of our platoons were on patrol from the north to the south coasts of Java. They had arrived at Ambarawa, sixty miles inland, when they were ambushed by a group of Nationalists and surrounded. Apparently they had not expected to meet any serious resistance and were quite lightly armed, with little ammunition. I was detailed to make the re-supply.

'I didn't have time to collect a full crew and took off with our signals officer, and a small squad of army types who would be pushing the supplies out. We found the location and let down to 300 feet over the small DZ, which was surrounded by the Indos. It took half a dozen runs to make the drop. We were sitting ducks and got peppered with rifle fire. We thanked our lucky stars they didn't have machine guns! The patrol fought its way out in the end.'

Christmas 1945 came and went and 31 Squadron was still busy in the Netherlands East Indies. In February, Norman and crew made five sorties to Bandoeng, 150 miles south-east of Batavia, taking supplies in and bringing back personnel:

'On landing for the fifth time, we were approached by an Indian Major, who told us that never before had any crew made five trips to his base in one day. He took us along to his quarters and produced a large bottle of brandy, which we helped him to empty. Well, it was so darned long since we'd seen brandy. The thirty Jap officers we were taking back to Batavia just had to wait.'

New crews were still arriving to replace those homeward bound. One of them came to grief late in the year:

'A Flying Officer and his crew were taking a load of soldiers from Batavia to Soerabaja when uncharacteristically the Dak developed engine trouble. They steadily lost height and were forced to crash-land, just three miles short of Kemajoran The captain managed that all right and no one was injured. They should have been picked up right away, but for some reason they weren't. The delay was tragic because armed locals surrounded them, took them down to the river where they lopped off their arms, legs and heads, and threw them into the water. When the military "Brass" got this news, they sent over a flight of fighters to shoot up the village, and anything or anyone in it. Needless to say, that was a strong reminder that we were still operating in hostile territory, regardless of the fact that the war in the Far East was supposedly over.'

By 4 March 1946, Flight Lieutenant Currell was at last 'tour expired'. He had put in a few minutes under 450 hours with 31 Squadron, and was rated an 'above average' pilot who had been accident free for the whole tour. He sailed on the Union Castle liner *Orontes*, which had been fitted out as a troopship. There were twenty-eight junior officers in one fairly large cabin:

'When it came to it, I was truly sorry to leave. I was enjoying my duties with the squadron, and missed the girls in the Happy World and the Dutch ladies of Batavia. On the two-week trip home, we were left to our own devices with no duties, and were fed regularly. But I did stir myself to make good friends with a girl from Chile who had been serving as a welfare hostess with TOC H. We arrived in Southampton a few days after Easter 1946.'

Nobby Knowles survived the horrors of Java and Sumatra and was shipped back to Singapore in March 1946. Benny Watts got back there a month later, able this time to hitch a ride in a Dakota, before being repatriated to England by ship through the Suez Canal.

At the time, Mountbatten wrote that he saw the Allied occupation of the Netherlands East Indies as the most complex and hazardous of his whole SEAC command. An interim Nationalist government was set up but it lacked control over the hotheads. The Dutch, the majority of whom had been born and then spent their entire lives in the colony, were aggressive and bitter. Hostilities were ferocious and the atrocities appalling. Trains and convoys were ambushed, POW camps stormed and thousands murdered on both sides.

Despite the difficulties, 100,000 internees were rescued and returned home, and tens of thousands of Japanese were disarmed. But despite handing over responsibility to the Dutch in May 1946, to keep some sort of order, the Allies remained in action through to the end of the year.

In this eighteen month extension of the south-east Asian conflict past VJ-Day, the RAF lost forty-two personnel killed or missing and suffered forty-one seriously injured. The contribution of 31 Squadron to the effort was 11,000 sorties flown, 127,800 passengers carried and 26,000 tons of freight delivered. On 30 September 1946, the squadron was disbanded in Java, having been in continuous existence, by curious coincidence, for just on thirty-one years.

Chapter 23

Civvy Street

After the war, the veterans mostly took up where they had left off, seeking normality after their ordeals in Burma.

George Hufflett went back to open-air work in Sussex, even managing a stint of brick making to strengthen his gammy right arm:

'I began to call on Mary, a girl who first caught my eye at school. She'd done her bit for the war effort, slaving away in a munitions factory up in Kingston-upon-Thames. I'd trudge over the fields to meet her at the Ram at Firle – her mother was the licensee there.

'Three years after I was demobbed, we were married. We moved into a semi-detached cottage in Alciston. It had electricity, but the water came from a well and there was a bucket toilet at the end of the garden – reminded me a bit of Burma, that did. We paid a rent of two shillings and sixpence a week. Later, when our young 'uns arrived, and the old fellow next door died, we took over the other half of the cottage and the rent went up to four bob. In one of the thatched cottages up the road we had that Kenneth Horne off the wireless – another war veteran he was, a wing commander in the RAF.

'In 1955, we moved into the Ram and two years after that Mary took over as licensee, just like her mother and grandmother before her. She was happy and so was I, behind the bar. It was a free house, the Ram. It was in a nice village, and had a good old garden, and all the brewery reps wanted to call. Harveys and Watneys we had – and Whitbread. Their rep was Jim Parkes, who'd just retired from cricket. He used to play for Sussex and England as wicketkeeper batsman. We got all the dressing-room gossip.

'Firle Estate owned the pub, still do, so we were always close to Lord Gage and his family up at Firle Place. We had a girl in to do the dishes and wait in the garden – hot pies we did, and bread and cheese, nothing too posh. It was a lovely time.'

Mary and George continued to run the Ram until 1985. Now in his 86th year, George is a respected village elder, always ready for a chat on his bench by the War Memorial. He is immediate past President of the Cricket Club and in 2005, when the Ram Inn re-opened for business after many thirsty weeks of closure for refurbishment, he was invited to pull the first pint, for Lord Gage. Since his encounter with the machine gun on Jail Hill he has had restricted feeling and movement in his right arm, but he could 'still pull a pint and take the money'. Apart from Burma, he has never travelled more than a few miles from his birthplace. He has a son and daughter and three grandchildren living nearby to listen to his stories. He thanks his lucky stars that that Japanese gunner was not a better shot.

After the war, John Hart did not go back to Oxo:

'They'd been very good to me. They'd made up my pension entitlement from when I passed twenty-one back in '42 and they didn't rush to stop the ten bob they were paying my mother. But after all that time outdoors in Burma, I couldn't deal with going back to work inside. So I got a job on the Thames barges, up at Hay's Wharf. After two years at that, I followed my father into the gasworks.

'But a lot of my mates in Rotherhithe were dockers – they were always giving me a load of palaver about how much money they were taking home and pushing me to join them. So in the end I did. It took me a good while, mind – the Docks turned out to be pretty much a closed shop. If my dad had been a docker it would have been easier – but he wasn't. They needed a bung of a hundred quid in the back pocket of the Union man to let me in – but I wasn't having any of that. In the end I wrote to the local MP, Bob Mellish, who was always in the papers, campaigning for democracy in the Docks and that sort of thing. I was lucky – he wrote to the National Dock Labour Board and got me through the gate. I worked up at Butlers Wharf on Tooley Street – right in the Pool of London, the Dockers' HQ, as it were. I used to unload Jaffa oranges, and reckoned I had it made.

'I hadn't though, not then. The system in the docks worked like this. If you weren't on the permanent staff, you turned up at the dock gates at a quarter to eight in the morning. If you were on what they called the Preferred List you were first in line for a day's work. For the rest – including me at the start – the gang foreman would walk along the line and give the nod to the geezers he liked the look of. "Casual", they called that system, and that's what it was. It began to crack in the late sixties when the docks were closing in central London and moving down to Tilbury. Then, they started to offer what they called 'turning-out money' to persuade us to go down-river – but I stayed where I was and in 1976 took the severance pay. It was good on the Docks while it lasted.

'My second wife, Vera, died five years ago. But I still live here, where we spent our last seven years together. I was born just down the street – apart from the time I spent in India and Burma I've lived all my life in Rotherhithe.'

He is, and always has been, a practising Roman Catholic. He went to a Catholic school and grew up in fear of religion and the priests:

'At Imphal they didn't have combined church services on a Sunday. But I found my religion a great help and a lot of my mates who said they were non-believers used to mutter prayers to some sort of God when things got dodgy. Anyhow, all the blokes kept their religion mostly to themselves – scared of having the mickey taken, probably. Each to his own, I say.

'I didn't see a single Jap in the campaign, and I never met

any POWs. But when I came back to Swan Lane Buildings, there was this bloke in the next flat who used to wake up screaming at night – he'd been in a Jap camp. And another thing – dockers used to black Japanese ships.

'It was lovely seeing my little girl playing with the other children in the street, hearing a band over in Southwark Park – all that sort of thing. But from time to time I did find myself missing the excitement and comradeship of Imphal, you know. Now I thank my Maker for sparing me.'

After demobilisation in 1947, Ken Brown went back to his father's newsagent's in Kemp Town:

'Somewhat to my surprise, they exchanged my Poona quick fire motorbike permit for a full driving licence – so I could drive the van. I also got hold of one of those BSA 500cc side-valve motorbikes, like the one I rode in Poona – cost me sixty quid. One day in the summer, I rode it down to Brighton Front – I fancied a dip in the briny. Not far out, I could see a lifeguard dinghy with a mate of mine rowing it, so I swam across and popped my head over the side. He had a girl with him, a real cracker – her name was Alice Townsend. We were married five years later, and stayed married for fifty-two years.

'When my dad retired I took over the shop, but I bought a little house for us both. We had a son and daughter who gave us six grandchildren and when my lovely Alice passed away four years ago, I stayed on here in the same house, where I can treasure her memory.

'I keep in touch with my south-east Asia memories through the Royal Signals Association and the Burma Stars of course. A mate and I set up the Brighton Branch forty-seven years ago. We needed a quorum of twenty members but at our first gathering were one short. So I signed up a willing chum who happened to be standing at the bar, and we were off. We had our first eight meetings after that at the Brighton Pavilion – really posh.

'We still have a pretty fair turnout at the Remembrance Day service. It's always good to see the ladies there, the ones who served in Burma – WAS(B)s, the Women's Auxiliary

Corps, the Red Cross and of course the Queen Alexandra's nurses.'

How does he feel about the religious aspects of Remembrance parades?

'It adds to the ceremonial really. I was brought up Church of England, but religion didn't do much for me in Burma. Although I have to say that in times of real danger I did find myself muttering the occasional prayer.'

Were the struggles and sacrifice in Burma worth it?

'In stopping the advance of a totalitarian power, yes, they certainly were. Of course, we all know now about the terrible events soon afterwards in India and Burma – but the Allied forces weren't to know that was going to happen. And think – if the Japs had got through to the subcontinent... Yes, it was all worth it. I'm proud to have been a part of it.'

Ken's near neighbour Arthur Watts – he left the 'Benny' behind in the Netherlands East Indies – went into farming:

'In April '46 I came home from Singapore by ship, through the Suez Canal, and by June, immediately after demob, I was married to Margery, my girl from before the war. Then I got on a two-year agricultural course at Monmouth. I found a job on a farm near Uckfield, and later another in Pulborough, where I was livestock manager. But things got tight in farming and in 1965 we moved to Brighton. I managed to get hired by a property company, and worked with them until I retired.'

Now a widower, he lives in a Brighton flat just around the corner from the Royal Sussex County Hospital – he finds he needs their services these days more often than he would like. He confesses to having mixed feelings about the Burma Campaign:

'Of course it was a triumph for the Allies in the end, but it was terrible the way the Nagas and the Shans and the other tribesmen were treated after the war. The Japs couldn't have been stopped without them – and then they were abandoned to the nationalist Burmese. At the same time, many of us felt that rather than fighting for King and Country we were liberating the mines, oil and paddy fields for the rich businessmen in India and London. I never could buy into the Establishment's line that God was on our side – but I was spared much of that, being so much away from main base and the Padres.'

Arthur is an active Burma Star, and has regularly attended the annual reunion of the 'Gold Stars'. For many years he was curator of 31 Squadron historical records, despite being sent by them on those landing ship ordeals. It would take a particularly heavy sea to sink Arthur Watts.

From Singapore, in December 1946 Nobby Knowles went with the Buffs to Hong Kong. By this time he had been promoted to corporal:

'We sailed in an Indian troopship, the SS *Dilwara*. We went aboard in the week before Christmas, and were given a fortnight's pay for the voyage – in Indian rupees. They were no effin' use so we'd changed them into Malay dollars – and spent them all, on the wharves of Singapore harbour. So we were skint on the voyage. We were still skint when we got to Hong Kong. The Field Cashier Officer, because it was Christmas, had forgotten to indent for our pay and it was close on another fortnight before we got any money. So what did we do? We did what soldiers always do – we sold our kit. The C/O, "Chunky Bruce", noticed a fair number of jungle-green tropical shirts appearing on the backs of the coolies at the barracks. He called a kit inspection, but of course all he got was, "One on, one in the dhobi, one lost in transit – Sir!" – and gave it up for a bad job.

'We were on garrison duties until November 1947, when, still only twenty-two, I sailed home to Southampton. By coincidence, it was on the same old *Dilwara*. I worked out that by then I'd done about 20,000 miles on troopships, landing craft and trooping flights – and I'd never once been sea or airsick.'

Eric – he too left his nickname abroad – arrived home at the beginning of 1948, the same year that the 2nd Battalion, the Buffs, was amalgamated with the 1st. The Shweli River and Myitson were its last battle honours:

'When I got back to Ilford – a full sergeant at just twenty-two – my dad as usual showed little emotion. But he did raise his eyebrows at the three stripes on my arm. At my holding barracks I was sent to deal with a detail of defaulters, "lifers" from the Far East. They trailed off the boat at Tilbury, all handcuffed together, bound for Fort Darland at Chatham. We put them in a metal cage on the back of a truck. When we got to the prison, and opened the cage door, blow me if they hadn't got the bloomin' cuffs off. It was a tense moment – but they were as good as gold. "You want to put these back on?" they said. So we did.

'I was posted to train National Servicemen in their six weeks of square-bashing in Cornwall. I stayed with the colours until the New Year of 1950, but then I left. I wanted to get married and I'd seen too many disastrous marriages in the army. A lot of raven-haired oriental beauties used to come on with, "Marry me, soldier and take me back to Blighty" – and they fell for it! I married the sister of a school friend and we had fifty-four years together.

'I went back to the *Daily Mirror*, and worked as Research Librarian. That was all right, but I once had to look up Java and Sumatra, and realised how much I was missing the buzz of military life. So I joined the Territorials, and got all the excitement I could have wanted. I had eighteen years with the Inns of Court Regiment, which was the Armoured Car Recce unit of 56th London Division. I finished up as a Squadron Sergeant Major.

'I retired in '86 and two years later moved to Coningsby, and the BBMF. I lost my wife four years ago, but my youngest daughter lives next door to me here. We had two other daughters and a son, and they gave us seven grand-children.

'I've always been active in the Church of England – by accident. My family were RC for generations but one day, my father woke up in hospital on the Western Front to find that he had been given C of E last rights. As he'd fallen for a Protestant girl, and wanted to marry her, he went along with it. In any event, he told me he'd lost his faith out there in the trenches, and I could believe that.

'I reckon that the Army's Church Parades turned a lot of people away from the Church. The Regimental Sergeant Major didn't help, with his "Take yer 'at orff in the 'ouse of Gawd". There was more chance of being put on jankers on Church Parade than any other occasion – maybe that was why Monty abolished them in '47. Anyway, the infantry-man's most passionate prayer was, "Please God, not in the eyes and not in the bollocks".'

Eric's duties at the Battle of Britain Memorial Flight keep him smart, and sharp. When his tour group comes to the Dakota, they certainly get their money's worth. His firsthand experience of active service in this famous aircraft is priceless and the fates are to be thanked that no Japanese or Indonesian Nationalist's bullet had his name on it.

With the unexpectedly early surrender of the Japanese, Henry Stock was not required to take part in Operation Zipper, and finished up in the Battalion Reserve in Madras, before being repatriated in January 1946:

'We were on the old *City of London*. She nearly didn't make it – bits fell off in the Med and we had to put in to Casablanca for repairs. After demob I went back to my wife and the Woolwich. I also took up again as a Scoutmaster – I'd been active in the movement before the war, and it was a great network to be in. You'd meet people you knew everywhere – in fact, at Pinwe I found myself fighting alongside a lad from my troop back home.'

Henry was with the Woolwich for a total of forty-four years. He lost his wife in 2005 after a marriage of sixty-seven years. He is very proud of the telegram the Queen sent them on their diamond anniversary. He enjoys the support of a large family –

seven grandchildren and at least four great-grandchildren (he's beginning to lose count). His home is alongside the busy A27 in Sompting, and when there, he goes shopping by bus, and welcomes visitors with tea and biscuits.

He has found it difficult to keep up with the changes of status of his Royal Sussex Regiment since the war, but the 'old boys' of the Shiny 9th Battalion, the 'Pinwe Club', still keep in touch, and enjoy an annual dinner. It was the sixtieth this year. He has considered moving to be nearer his eldest son in Hampshire but he's afraid he might miss his old pals too much. For them and his family it was a blessing the Japanese spared Henry at Pinwe.

The day after arriving home in Southampton in December 1945, Derrick Hull went to the railway station to meet Vera, who was on a weekend pass from the WAAFs:

'It was perishing cold, so I got myself wrapped up in my old man's scarf and gloves. Would you believe it? I was clobbered by an RAF Policeman for being improperly dressed. There were a few choice words exchanged I can tell you – from one corporal to another, you understand.

'I was posted to 13 Maintenance Unit at Henlow and worked in the Instrument Section – all run by WAAFs by then. I worked on artificial horizons. Boring stuff – I much preferred aircraft.

'Vera and I got married in May '46 and after our honeymoon in the Isle of Wight, I was posted to Kemble, near Stroud – an assignment to fit autopilots in Lancasters. But after a couple of months, in August, when I'd done nearly 200 of them, they started breaking the rest up for scrap. So it was back to Henlow.

'My time-expired date was coming up and I was promised sergeant's stripes if I'd sign on again, but it was a certainty I'd be sent overseas and, being married, I declined. I was demobbed in October '46.

'Jobs weren't easy to come by and I didn't find one until well into the next year – as a neon-sign glass bender in Brighton. That lasted until '51, when Stafford Cripps stopped the import of the necessary glass from the

Continent. That probably saved my life – there was a lot of mercury in the tubing and I'd already been working with it four years. In fact I did take very ill, and had a couple of years in and out of hospital, before getting a job in Shoreham Council's ratings department. I was there for ten years and then in '63 I joined the gas industry, and worked in administration until I retired in 1987.'

Derrick, very recently widowed, lives in the house in Hove which he and Vera bought in 1964. The furniture, and a magnificent teak model ship on the landing window sill, bear witness to his hobby, working with wood – an inheritance perhaps from his Lyndhurst forester ancestors.

What did the heroics of the Burma Campaign, and the tragic loss of life, achieve?

'They stopped the Japs – that's all. But I haven't buried the memories of my time in the forces. I'm a life member of both the Royal Air Force and Burma Star Associations and I've scrapbooks full of mementoes of Burma – and a daughter, three grandchildren and two great-grandchildren to share them with. That's a priceless gift, after all the close calls of my life.'

Derrick's brother Richard arrived home in the New Year of 1947, and after twenty-eight days' disembarkation leave he was only three months from demob:

'They posted me to RAF Thorney Island, a smashing station on the south coast, near Pompey, where I worked in a radio transmitter station. I got myself a motorbike, smuggled out the odd gallon or two of petrol from the emergency generators, and had a lot of fun. The brakes on the bike weren't great and I had a close call on Portsdown Hill when I found myself sailing straight through a full-blown Naval Parade. The 'Big Brass' on the review stand weren't exactly pleased to see me – but I went through so quick they couldn't catch me. I didn't even have time to salute!

'In April '47 I had to trail up to Warrington to get demobbed. I went back to the *Echo* and enjoyed myself playing cricket and golf, and sailing, and then I met Jill and we were married in '68. I stayed with the *Echo* until my retirement in 1990.

'It's a funny thing, fate. My father served in the Royal Bucks Hussars in the First World War and took part in one of the last British cavalry charges, against the Turkish guns at El Muhgar in 1917. He survived the carnage of that and was put on a troopship for the Western Front. But in the Med, they were torpedoed, and as the ship was going down, a Japanese destroyer appeared. Its sailors stripped off and plunged into the water to the rescue. Thirty years later I was dropping ammo into the jungle to help our lads to kill as many Japs as possible. Yet my old man owed his life to them, and therefore, so do I – as well as our son and daughter, two granddaughters and two grandsons. The irony of it all.'

On his demob in June 1946, Peter Bray's experience and flying hours qualified him for a 'B' Air Line Transport Pilot's (ALTP) Licence, and he was able straight away to join BEA which later became British Airways European Division:

'I went on to get my Navigation Certificate, Second Class, at Hamble, and could convert my licence to a full ALTP. I went back to the Dakota, flying out of Northolt, and then progressed through all the fleets. After the Dak it was its replacement, the Vickers Viking, and then on to the first turboprop, the Airspeed Ambassador. We took Winston Churchill to Paris in that. Then I converted to the Vickers Viscount and Vanguard, and finally the Trident, introducing automatic landing. I retired in June 1974, with 20,000 flying hours. I was proud that 2,000 of those were on the Burma Front.'

Phyllis had been laid off from her work at the Cirencester post office when she married, and Peter hadn't had the time to write many letters, but she survived the isolation of a wartime wife – and the stresses of marriage to an airline pilot. They had three children who have given them five grandchildren and three great-grandchildren.

Peter has recently made a visit to the Bauhaus-designed family house in Weimar, for the first time after sixty-eight years, and now has a project helping the current owner to restore it to its original state, even replacing the china and glass (there is a Weimar crystal bowl in the Shoreham flat) and the wallpaper (Peter has a picture of the original in the living-room).

What were his thoughts on the Burma Campaign?

'I have to say I enjoyed it. I was too busy to be downhearted and the flying was exhilarating. We didn't get much time for leisure, but Darjeeling was memorable, as was Vera Lynn's visit in March '44. Of course I missed Phyllis and was delighted to come home, but the campaign was after all a triumph. It was a lesson in the advantages of the Army and the Air Force working together – I still remember the Army Liaison Officer on 31 Squadron, a chap by the name of Osborne. Without that sort of cooperation we would never have managed it. Yes, a triumph.'

When the *Orontes* docked in Southampton, just after Easter 1946, Norman Currell and his travelling companions took the train to London for demob:

'It was perishing cold for us after months in the tropics. But Easter was the cut-off point for the heating in the carriages and that was that – we froze, and all of us came down with colds. What with that and the prospect of a crowded job market for returned men, the euphoria of victory soon wore off. Anyway, the conflict in Java and Sumatra was pretty much invisible – the people and politicians had other things on their minds.

'I got a warm welcome from my family and friends but had no hope of a job, and I decided I'd have better chances in Canada. But the ships were also crowded, with Canadians wanting to get home. However, my years in flying training out there did the trick and I was given just ten days' notice of a berth on the *Aquitania*. After hurried farewells, I sailed for Montreal. On the ship there were all of 1,300 British war brides – on one full deck, and heavily guarded.

'I made my way back to Moose Jaw, and then on to Vancouver where I tried the commercial fishing industry, without much success. Then in January '47 I found my niche – I joined the Western Oil Company in Saskatchewan and never looked back except once when, soon after the war, I received notice of the award of a Distinguished Flying Cross, DFC, for "keenness and courage in supply dropping operations in Burma". The citation also said that in all my missions I had never brought a load back. That made my chest swell all right.'

He prospered in the oil industry until his retirement in 1979, when he moved to Langley, British Columbia, where he now lives with his fifth wife, Helena. For years he had put memories of the Far East campaigns well behind him, but in his 95th year, it has all come flooding back:

'I reckon the British Commonwealth Air Training Scheme was an outstanding contribution to the Allies' war effort – the thirty months I was in it exceeded my wildest dreams and I thank Canada for the experience. I also thank the fates for steering me away from Bomber Command. You know, we go on about the Jap suicide pilots but the way our boys were sent in such numbers to their deaths over Germany came close to kamikaze.

'I bear no grudge against the Japanese as a race. Most of the ordinary people had no idea what was going on – all that business with a divine Emperor was just another example of the establishment using enforced beliefs to manipulate the masses. Many nations have done that, including the British with its established church, and still do.'

He was for many years active in the Burma Stars in Langley, and for his work as Branch Secretary, has been rewarded with a life membership. He has the support of his two sons and their wives, and two grandchildren. But they live 3,000 miles away in Ontario – a big country, Canada. His wife's son and daughter, with their children and grandchildren, live closer. They have to come to see him for he doesn't travel far any more. He gets out shopping now and then on his electric scooter, but his car is as much a thing of the past as is his beloved Dakota.

After his demob in 1946, Colin Lynch received three months' full RAF pay, and enjoyed an allowance from home in India. But he lacked for contacts. Even some old friends from India who had promised him lodgings found their house was after all, too full and he found himself standing in the rain in Bexhill-on-Sea with a tin trunk and a bed-roll:

> 'Charlie Mann came to the rescue. He had also opted for demob in England and had a spare bed in his room in London's Northfields. But I felt like a fish out of water up there and after three months I managed to get a small room of my own, in Ealing. I had no plans about what to do for a living. It was mighty cold, and I was glad I'd kept hold of my old RAF greatcoat. It didn't help my peace of mind to read in the papers about the horrors of Partition in India, and the troubles my family were going through.
>
> 'Then, along with several other ex-servicemen, I got on a two-year graphic design course at Hammersmith School of Art – more girls, some studying, most enjoyable. I was expected to look for a job in commercial art, but the Ad-Industry wasn't booming just then. Lady Luck stepped in again when a fellow student came back from an interview with Harold Weinberg's Ad Agency in Fleet Street, saying it didn't suit him, might it suit me? I went along, and got the job. It didn't pay much, but it was work. And I liked it, and did well. I was there for seven years.
>
> 'At Easter in '49, I met Jean at a dance in Ealing Broadway. That was a bit of luck, too – she'd had a narrow escape back in 1940. She was on the list of children to be evacuated to Canada on the *City of Benares*. But her mum couldn't get her father's signature on the necessary form and she missed the boat – which was torpedoed. The total death roll was 294 – including eighty-three of the ninety children on board. We were married in 1952, when I was twenty-nine and she was just twenty.'

After Weinberg, Colin moved to Central Art Studios, went freelance and joined NPF Design. He has been freelance ever since.

He and Jean live in a bungalow, appropriately called Sherwood, in Hillingdon, close to their daughter and son and their families. Jean says that for years, Colin would not talk about his time in Burma. Then, after he finally retired from fulltime freelance artwork, he began to open up. He has contributed to *Star News* and goes to 31 Squadron and Sherwood College reunions.

He becomes angry when talk turns to medals:

'My 2,000 hours in the frontline of air supply earned me a Burma Star campaign medal, no more. But then, it was well known that the handing out of DFMs and DFCs was something of a lottery.'

He gets even angrier when reminded of the sufferings of the Allied prisoners under the Japanese. His brother Vic was captured early in the Burma Campaign and only just survived. Overall, one in four of the prisoners died, from malnutrition, dysentery, malaria, cholera, beri-beri, exhaustion – and beheading and other unimaginably horrific deaths.

Colin shows the scars across his ribs where the Japanese shrapnel hit him. A dozen bits were taken out in Assam, and in a second operation, in England, four more. But his most harrowing memories of the 1940s are not of Burma, but of the horrors his family suffered after he had left India, in the terrible events of Partition:

'My family came to England two years after the war. They weren't chucked out – they just found it impossible to stay. My dad was being side-lined by the Indianisation of jobs on the railways, and he went to work every day past banners proclaiming, "Jia Hind!" As it got worse, they moved their possessions to storage in Bombay. There, everything got stolen except for the sewing machine – and the piano, but that was dropped in transit and its back was broken.

'After the war my nanny had married a British soldier.

They ambushed the train taking her to Bombay and the boat to Blighty, and slaughtered all the whites. The same thing happened to the boss of my ITW. That was on the North-West Frontier – rebels murdered the whole family.

'All our servants were Hindu, save for the Muslim tailor, Darzi. Sikhs were rampaging in the streets of Delhi, looking for Muslims, so my mum kept him hidden in the garage. The Government were collecting Muslims in a refugee centre, for deportation to Pakistan – Darzi decided to go with them. With tears in his eyes at leaving, he walked through the garden gates. He got no more than thirty yards down the road – and was shot.'

In London, Colin's parents took a house near Hanger Lane, Ealing. His father, who had had status, security and respect in India, had lost his pension – so he took a job cleaning hospital floors. Colin's mother died aged sixty-two and his father at eighty-six.

With his three brothers, four sisters and so many relations and friends all born and bred in India, Colin has always thought of that country as home – the home where his heart is. He rages at the injustice of fate:

'Looking back, I miss the close family life, and the many friends that we had wherever we went in that vast country of fantastic mountains, hills, valleys, rivers, lakes, jungles and plains. It's clear – Indian independence was forced through by the politicians, Indian and British. Had it been put to a referendum the people would almost certainly have rejected it. India was a terrific place, and in good financial shape – the stock market had remained strong throughout the war. I used to spend any leave I got in Delhi – I had a girl-friend there. It was a great place – dances, concerts and sports of all sorts. There were Scottish clubs, and Irish clubs. There was very little class-snobbery – except in the British military. All the races tolerated all the others – even the Hindus and Muslims. If only it could have stayed that way, but of course, with Partition, it didn't.

'So, what were all our efforts for? All those lives sacrificed?

'We kept the Japs out of India, and drove them out of Burma all right. But after all that, there was so much suffering and loss – on both sides. Tragic. Such a waste.'

Vera Lynn was not immune from the mental pressures of peace. A few months after the end the war, she and Harry had a daughter, Virginia, and soon after the birth, following a celebration concert at the Royal Albert Hall, she surprised and shocked her public by announcing she was to retire.

But her retirement didn't last long. As early as Christmas 1946 she'd begun a limited return to recording, and by the end of 1947 she was working again, touring the variety circuit and gaining another BBC radio programme. In one month of 1952, three of her records were in the top twelve in the fledgling New Musical Express charts. In the same year she became the first British singer to top the American charts – for nine whole weeks. They loved her in Holland, where they'd listened to her in the war, and in Germany too, where they called her 'the lady with steel in her voice'. In the fifties she broke into television, and remained a favourite for three decades. She received an OBE in 1969, and in 1975 was made a Dame Commander of the British Empire. Not bad for a little girl from East Ham.

A few days before her ninetieth birthday, Dame Vera Lynn sits in a golf club restaurant not far from her home in Ditchling, where she has lived for forty years. A widow now, she is a local celebrity – the dining golfers treat her with affectionate respect, and the waitresses form a mini guard of honour as she arrives.

She says her tour of Burma was ground-breaking:

'Other stars went out after me – Elsie and Doris Waters arrived in Shillong with their "Gert and Daisy" act as I left.'

She's too polite to mention that Noel Coward went too, and famously flopped with the bemused Yanks at Ledo.

She was at all but two of the forty-nine annual Burma Star Association celebrations at the Royal Albert Hall, and also sang at commemorations of the 40th anniversary of D-Day and the 50th of the outbreak of the Second World War. In 2005, she spoke on behalf of veterans at the 60th anniversary of VE Day:

'Perhaps the most moving moment of all though, was when I went on *This is Your Life*. One of the Burma boys who turned up to meet me was the surviving one of the two lads I'd sung to in that tent in Dimapur.'

Dame Vera's daughter says that her mother was of 'the Churchill breed' and, as she proved beyond measure in Burma, 'ready for anything'.

That could well stand as the motto for all twelve of these veterans, who made it through the mud, swamps, disease and bullets to live out their days in peace.

Postlude

In the 1970s, Arthur Watts made a trip back to Kohima with Margery, and was dismayed to discover that the Indians had made it a controlled zone. It needed the intervention of Jim Callaghan, who, as Prime Minister, was visiting India at the time, to get them permission to go there. It was worth the effort. They found it almost impossibly moving to stand by the memorial stone, on Garrison Hill, and read the now famous inscription:

> When you go home
> Tell them of us and say
> For your tomorrow
> We gave our today

Below is written:

> In memory
> of the men
> of the
> 2nd Division
> who fell in the battle for Kohima
> and in the fighting for the Imphal Road
> April 1944 to June 1944

The monument, carved from local Naga stone, stands on the site of the District Commissioner's old bungalow and tennis court, in the cemetery of the 2nd British Division with the graves of nearly 1,400 men. Among them lie two soldiers who won the

Victoria Cross at the battle, in which the Allies had 4,000 casualties and the Japanese, 5,000.

Of the 330,000 Japanese soldiers who went to Burma, over 200,000 never returned home. In the retreat and the subsequent Burma Campaign, the Allies lost some 15,000 combatants – roughly one in thirteen of the million who served there. Just under 5,000 of those were of United Kingdom origin, 7,500 from the British Indian Army and the remainder, Gurkha and African troops. In addition, there were over 100,000 Allied personnel listed as 'missing and POW'. These figures can be read alongside the number of United Kingdom citizens killed in Hitler's air raids, over 60,000, and of Burmese civilians who perished, a quarter of a million.

Perla Gibson, the 'Lady in White', sang from the Durban quays to more than 1,000 troopships and 350 hospital ships. A year after her death in 1971, just before her eighty-third birthday, a stone cairn with a bronze plaque to her memory was erected on the North Pier, where she had serenaded the boys. It was donated by the men of the Royal Navy. In 1995, a statue of Perla was unveiled in the Ocean Terminal Building by the Queen.

In May 2007, a piece appeared in *The Times* headlined: 'India hopes old jungle trail can be a new road to riches'. India had begun reconstructing the 1,000-mile Stilwell Road connecting it to China via Burma, more than six decades after it was built. Winston Churchill is quoted as describing the road as 'an immense, laborious task, unlikely to be finished until the need for it has passed'. He was almost right as the road delivered a lifeline to the Chinese nationalist forces for just ten months, before it was engulfed by jungle and mudslides. China is so keen to reopen the road, which will reduce their reliance on the transport of goods by sea through the Malacca Straits, that they have already converted their stretch to a six-lane highway, as well as helping the Burmese to rebuild much of their section. India has finally given in to pressure and agreed to resurrect its thirty-eight mile stretch. 'We expect the work to be completed by March 2009,' says the Minister of Road Transport. The Ledo Road will be back in business.

Colin Lynch's brother, Vic has some commemorative brass nails from the Burma-Siam railway – the 'Death Railway', which was completed in October 1943, and continually attacked and disabled by the RAF thereafter. Running from Bangkok to Rangoon, it is 258 miles in length. It was built over eighteen months by the forced labour of 100,000 Allied prisoners of war and 60,000 Asian slave labourers and, of those, it claimed 16,000 Allied and 9,000 Asian lives. It was tragic that its construction was necessary only because of the success British submarines were having in restricting Japanese shipping, en route for Burma through the Straits of Malacca. It was a cruel irony that in planning it, the Japanese used surveys of the route made by the British before the war. Today, just eighty miles are still in use – the rest has been abandoned.

In the war in south-east Asia, 5,100 RAF men became prisoners of the Japanese, mostly captured in Java and Sumatra. Of those, 1,700 died in captivity, exactly one third. Of the 10,000 who fell into German hands, just 152 died.

As is normal in war, the combatants can see little more than their own corner – the next mountain climb or bamboo thicket, the next water or meal. So it is perhaps no surprise that none of these veterans once mentioned the events on the seas around Burma.

The first British Royal Naval Squadron reappeared in Ceylon in January 1944, with three capital ships and two aircraft carriers. That they were there at all was due to the escape of the British East Indies Fleet from Colombo and Tricomalee as the Japanese advanced in 1942, and that in turn owed a lot to RAF Catalina amphibians that shadowed the enemy ships as they approached.

When they returned to the Indian Ocean, and the Japanese in their turn retreated to the Pacific action, the Allied fleet ruled some 7 million square miles of sea. It was a crucial time, as the counterattack was being launched on three fronts. The Navy was in the van in the coastal assaults, and kept the Japanese sea lines of communication in considerable check. It helped that the Americans sank 750 Japanese cargo ships en route for Burma, in the Pacific. A Japanese division needed 100 tons of foodstuffs every six days – and they didn't get it.

It could be said that in 1944 and '45, sea power laid the foundation of Allied victory. The soldiers, airmen and the Dakotas then won the campaign.

In Burma, as everywhere else during the Second World War, the DC-3 military versions, the C-47 and the Dakota were as ubiquitous in the air and on the airfields as the VW Beetle was later to become on the world's roads. During the war, more than 10,000 were manufactured at the Douglas factories. Of those, 2,000 were delivered to the RAF, and 700 to Russia via Anchorage and Siberia. By mid-1944, they were coming off the production line at a rate of one every thirty-four minutes, and by the time peace was declared, there were more of the type flying than of any other in history. Its ruggedness was legendary. In one extraordinary incident in the Pacific, even after a Japanese Kamikaze pilot had taken the top off the fuselage of a C-47, it and the crew made it back to base. It was designed to carry twenty-four passengers maximum. In one evacuation in Burma – of Lieutenant Colonel Jimmy Doolittle and the survivors of his Tokyo raid – a Dakota took off with seventy-four men all at once, and delivered them safely.

General Eisenhower listed the aircraft among his four vital bits of kit – the others were the bulldozer, the Jeep (both of which were carried by the Dakota) and the 2½-ton truck. It was not at first intended or designed for combat – like most Burma veterans it was originally an ordinary citizen.

Production ceased in 1946, but the DC-3 flew on – and on. USAF C-47s and RAF Dakotas initiated the Berlin Airlift, their floor panels sealed with plasticine in an attempt to keep the coal dust out. The US Navy flew them off the carrier *Philippine Sea* in support of Admiral Bird's Antarctic research. They were still available for Korea, and for Indo-China – first with the French Armée de l'Air and then as an American gunship. They ended up being in service with fifty air forces around the world.

DC-3s were used for tasks as varied as drug smuggling, gun running, oil pollution control, surveying, sky-diving – and for at least one airborne wedding. In 1951 a BEA stretched version became the first airliner to be powered by turboprop engines – Rolls-Royce Darts. DC-3s were carrying fare paying passengers until at least the mid-1960s. In December 1978, one splendid old stager had clocked up over 80,000 airframe hours, carried over 1 million passengers and flown 12½ million miles. The Dutch Dakota Association still has two flying and plans to keep at least one of them airworthy for the 75th Anniversary, on 17 December 2010, of the first DC-2 flight.

In America, the DC-3 transformed air travel. In Burma, the C-47 and the Dakota then went on to transform air supply and troop movement, and assure the Allies of final victory.

Bibliography

Air Staff Headquarters, ACSEA, *Air Transport Operations on the Burma Front*, New Delhi, July 1944

Anon, *Wings of the Phoenix: The official story of the Air War in Burma during WW2*, HMSO, 1949

Fergusson, Bernard, *Beyond the Chindwin*, William Collins & Sons Ltd, 1945

Franks, Norman L.R., *The Air Battle of Imphal*, William Kimber, 1985

Lynn, Vera, *Vocal Refrain: An Autobiography*, W.H. Allen, 1975

— with Robin Cross, *We'll Meet Again: A Personal and Social History of World War Two*, Sidgwick & Jackson, 1989

Owen, Lieutenant Colonel Frank OBE, *Burma, a miracle in military achievement*, SEAC Newspapers, The Statesman Press Calcutta (1945)

— *The Campaign in Burma*, Her Majesty's Stationery Office, 1946

Pearcy, Arthur Jnr, *The Dakota*, Ian Allen, 1972

Pearson, Michael, *The Burma Air Campaign 1941-1945*, Pen & Sword Books, 2006

Probert, Air Commodore Henry, *The Forgotten Air Force: The Royal Air Force in the War against Japan 1941-1945*, Brassey's, 1995

Saunders, Hilary St G., Royal Air Force 1939-45, Volume III – The Fight is Won, HMSO, 1975

Slim, Field Marshal Sir William, *Defeat Into Victory*, Cassel & Co. Ltd, 1956

The Royal Air Force Historical Society, *The RAF and the Far East War 1941-1945*, The Royal Air Force Historical Society, 1995

Warwick, Nigel W.M., *Constant Vigilance: The RAF Regiment in the Burma Campaign*, Pen & Sword Aviation, 2007

Williams, Flight Lieutenant Douglas, *194 Squadron Royal Air Force – The Friendly Firm*, Merlin Books Ltd, 1987

Index